Spanish Verbs For Dummies®

Subject Pronouns for All Occasions

	Singular	Plural
First person	yo = I	nosotros = we (male or mixed group)
		nosotras = we (female)
Second person familiar	tú = you	vosotros = you (male or mixed group)
		vosotras = you (female)
Third person	él = he	ellos = they (male or mixed group)
	ella = she	ellas = they (female)
Second person formal	Ud. = you	Uds. = you

Present Tense Endings for Regular Verbs

All three verb types have the same present tense **yo** ending. Also, **-er** and **-ir** verbs are conjugated the same except for their **nosotros** and **vosotros** forms.

-ar verbs	
yo -o	nosotros/as -amos
tú -as	vosotros/as - áis
el, ella -a Ud.	ellos/as -an Uds.

-er verbs	
yo -o	nosotros/as -emos
tú -es	vosotros/as -éis
el, ella -e Ud.	ellos/as -en Uds.

-ir verbs	
yo -o	nosotros/as -imos
tú -es	vosotros/as -ís
el, ella -e Ud.	ellos/as -en Uds.

For Dummies: Bestselling Book Series for Beginners

Spanish Verbs For Dummies®

The Six Remaining Simple Tenses

Regular -ar verbs — **hablar** = to speak

	Stem	yo	tú	él, ella, Ud.	nosotros/as	vosotros/as	ellos/as, Uds.
Imperfect	habl +	-aba	-abas	-aba	-ábamos	-abais	-aban
Preterit	habl +	-é	-aste	-ó	-amos	-asteis	-aron
Future	hablar +	-é	-ás	-á	-emos	-éis	-án
Conditional	hablar +	-ía	-ías	-ía	-íamos	-íais	-ían
Present Subjunctive	habl +	-e	-es	-e	-emos	-éis	-en
Imperfect Subjunctive	habl +	-ara	-aras	-ara	-áramos	-arais	-aran
Imperfect Subjunctive (alternative)	habl +	-ase	-ases	-ase	-ásemos	-aseis	-asen

Note: The first imperfect subjunctive form is the one most commonly used.

Regular -er and -ir verbs — **comer** = to eat; **vivir** = to live

	Stem	yo	tú	él, ella, Ud.	nosotros/as	vosotros/as	ellos/as, Uds.
Imperfect	com/viv +	-ía	-ías	-ía	-íamos	-íais	-ían
Preterit	com/viv +	-í	-iste	-ió	-imos	-isteis	-ieron
Future	comer/vivir +	-é	-ás	-á	-emos	-éis	-án
Conditional	comer/vivir +	-ía	-ías	-ía	-íamos	-íais	-ían
Present Subjunctive	com/viv +	-a	-as	-a	-amos	-áis	-an
Imperfect Subjunctive	com/viv +	-iera	-ieras	-iera	-iéramos	-ierais	-ieran
Imperfect Subjunctive (alternative)	com/viv +	-iese	-ieses	-iese	-iésemos	-ieseis	-iesen

Forming Present Participles (-ing) for Regular Verbs

Verb Ending	Rule	Verb	Present participle
-ar	stem + -ando	**hablar** = to speak	**hablando** = speaking
-er or -ir	stem + -iendo	**comer** = to eat **vivir** = to live	**comiendo** = eating **viviendo** = living

Forming Past Participles (-ed, -en) for Regular Verbs

Verb Ending	Rule	Verb	Past Participle
-ar	stem + -ado	**hablar** = to speak	**hablado** = spoken
-er or -ir	stem + -ido	**comer** = to eat **vivir** = to live	**comido** = eaten **vivido** = lived

For Dummies: Bestselling Book Series for Beginners

Spanish Verbs

FOR

DUMMIES®

Spanish Verbs
FOR
DUMMIES®

by Cecie Kraynak

WILEY

Wiley Publishing, Inc.

Spanish Verbs For Dummies®

Published by
Wiley Publishing, Inc.
111 River St.
Hoboken, NJ 07030-5774
www.wiley.com

Copyright © 2006 by Wiley Publishing, Inc., Indianapolis, Indiana

Published simultaneously in Canada

For general information on our other products and services, please contact our Customer Care Department within the U.S. at 800-762-2974, outside the U.S. at 317-572-3993, or fax 317-572-4002.

For technical support, please visit www.wiley.com/techsupport.

Wiley also publishes its books in a variety of electronic formats. Some content that appears in print may not be available in electronic books.

Library of Congress Control Number: 2005936632

ISBN-13: 978-0-471-76872-2

ISBN-10: 0-471-76872-3

Manufactured in the United States of America

10 9 8 7 6 5 4 3 2 1

1B/RR/QR/QW/IN

WILEY

About the Author

While some people get revved up at car races and others ride the wild waves of the stock market, Cecie Kraynak gets her jollies traveling to Spanish-speaking countries, chatting it up with complete strangers, and haggling with the local merchants.

Cecie inherited her love of Spanish language and culture from her mother, Jo Anne Howard, also a Spanish major, who cultivated Cecie's innate interest and encouraged her to travel and study abroad. From the heartland of Crawfordsville, Indiana, Cecie first set out to study at the University of the Americas in Cholua, Mexico, and later spent her junior year abroad at the Universidad Complutense in Madrid, Spain. She earned her Bachelor's degree in Spanish and secondary education in 1980 from Purdue University, and also received her Master's degree in Spanish literature from Purdue. During her grad school years, Cecie taught Spanish to undergraduates and served as the graduate assistant for Purdue's summer study program in Mexico City.

After graduating in 1983, Cecie began what was to become a 20-year career teaching Spanish to junior high and high school students. She continues to teach and travel and has served as a consultant on several Spanish learning guides, including *Teach Yourself Spanish in 24 Hours* (MacMillan) and *Spanish for Healthcare Professionals* (Barron's).

Dedication

To Joe, without whom this book would never have made it to press; to my mother, who shared her love of Spanish with me in the first place; and to my high school Spanish teacher, Marilyn Britton, who gave me such a fantastic foundation in Spanish grammar and usage.

Acknowledgments

Thanks to Mikal Belicove for choosing me to write this book and working closely with me during the initial stages to formulate a vision for the book. Thanks also go to project editors Jennifer Connolly and Traci Cumbay for carefully shaping the manuscript and shepherding the text through production, and to Neil Johnson and Danielle Voirol, copy editors, for purging the manuscript of any typos and ugly grammatical errors. Special thanks to technical editor Matthew Philbrick for diligently checking my presentation of the topic for technical accuracy and ensuring that the material was presented in an easily understood format. Last but not least, thanks to la Sra. Cindy Franklin, Spanish Teacher at Speedway High School, for generously sharing her resources with me and to Elise Eggers for contributing her talents and expertise.

Publisher's Acknowledgments

We're proud of this book; please send us your comments through our Dummies online registration form located at www.dummies.com/register/.

Some of the people who helped bring this book to market include the following:

Acquisitions, Editorial, and Media Development

Project Editors: Jennifer Connolly, Traci Cumbay

Acquisitions Editors: Mikal Belicove, Mike Lewis

Copy Editors: Neil Johnson, Danielle Voirol

Editorial Program Assistant: Courtney Allen

Technical Editor: Matthew Philbrick

Editorial Supervisor: Carmen Krikorian

Editorial Manager: Michelle Hacker

Editorial Assistants: Hanna Scott, David Lutton

Cartoons: Rich Tennant (www.the5thwave.com)

Composition Services

Project Coordinator: Adrienne Martinez

Layout and Graphics: Denny Hager, Stephanie D. Jumper, Erin Zeltner

Proofreaders: Leeann Harney, Jessica Kramer, Arielle Meunelle

Indexer: Johnna VanHoose

Publishing and Editorial for Consumer Dummies

Diane Graves Steele, Vice President and Publisher, Consumer Dummies

Joyce Pepple, Acquisitions Director, Consumer Dummies

Kristin A. Cocks, Product Development Director, Consumer Dummies

Michael Spring, Vice President and Publisher, Travel

Kelly Regan, Editorial Director, Travel

Publishing for Technology Dummies

Andy Cummings, Vice President and Publisher, Dummies Technology/General User

Composition Services

Gerry Fahey, Vice President of Production Services

Debbie Stailey, Director of Composition Services

Contents at a Glance

Table of Contents

Introduction

*V*erbs seem simple enough, right? They're action words. They describe what's happening, what happened, or what will happen. In practice, however, they become a little more complicated. They change depending on the time the action occurred, the being or number of beings performing the action, the likelihood that an action or condition can occur, and whether the action is a statement, question, or command.

In your native language, you automatically select the correct verb form without thinking twice about it, but when you're picking up a new language, you need to figure out how to *conjugate* the different verb types so that they agree with the subject of the sentence — I; you (singular); he, she, or it; we; you (plural); or they — and express the action in the right tense — past, present, or future, just to name a few. I'd name them all right here, but Spanish has a total of 14 tenses. And if that isn't enough to drive you batty, some Spanish verb stems even change their spellings.

Yep, Spanish verbs are pretty much out to get you. Fortunately, *Spanish Verbs For Dummies* is here to help you survive the onslaught and make sense of the confusing rules and regulations and to drill you on the most common exceptions. Each chapter is packed with examples, conjugation charts, and plenty of exercises to drive the point home.

This book is your opportunity to prove to yourself that you've mastered Spanish verbs and can use them in a sentence. With *Spanish Verbs For Dummies*, a little practice reading conjugation charts, and a pencil or pen, you're well-prepared to tackle even the most irregular verbs in the Spanish language.

About This Book

Spanish Verbs For Dummies is a refresher course, reference book, and workbook all rolled into one and seasoned with just a dash of humor. Each chapter addresses a tense by showing you how to form it (in Spanish, of course), illustrates how to use the tense in context, and then tests your mettle with exercises that help you determine whether you've mastered the lesson.

Most of the exercises you meet along the way are true/false questions or actual translations. I could've thrown in some multiple choice or matching exercises, but in Spanish, you typically find out very little from such activities, so I decided to stick with something a little more challenging.

One nice thing about this workbook and other *For Dummies* books is that you can choose to work all the way through the book from Chapter 1 to the very end, or you can skip around however you like. If you've already mastered a particular tense, for example, you don't have to spend time reviewing it and scribbling answers in the book. That way, you can devote more time to the conjugations that are most perplexing. Dive in wherever you want, and if you need to swim back to shore, that's fine, too.

Conventions Used in This Book

I used several conventions in this book to present the information in a consistent format. As you work through the book, you may bump into the following items:

- **Conjugation boxes:** As you begin to use this book, you will no doubt notice that I chose a rather conventional method to introduce the different verb conjugations. I use what I refer to as the *conjugation box*, which looks like this:

pedir (e-i) = to ask for	
yo pido	nosotros/as pedimos
tú pides	vosotros/as pedís
él, ella pide Ud.	ellos/as piden Uds.

  This handy little tool acts like a mental billboard. It displays the **Spanish verb,** its English meaning, and then conjugates the verb, presenting the three singular conjugations in the left column and the three plural conjugations in the right column.

- **Vocabulary chart:** Vocabulary charts provide a quick rundown of common words or expressions typically providing the **Spanish word** in the left column with its English equivalent in the right column. In some cases, the charts contain additional columns to illustrate different forms, such as a present participle.

- **Instructions for practice activities:** I include instructions for each set of practice activities. The instructions are intended to be short and sweet, so you can quickly proceed to the task at hand.

- **Answer keys:** At the end of each chapter is an Answer Key that provides the correct answers to all practice activities within the chapter. In some cases where you answer **cierto** (true) or **falso** (false), I simply provide a translation of the statements in question, because technically no answer is right or wrong.

You're likely to spot the following abbreviations, as well. Don't let them throw you off course.

- sing. (singular)
- pl. (plural)
- m. or masc. (masculine)
- f. or fem. (feminine)

Each chapter of this book begins with a concise explanation of the topic at hand — typically a specific Spanish verb tense conjugation, just in case you need a brief refresher. However, this book assumes that you've already had *some* exposure to the topic, either in a class or in another book, such as *Spanish For Dummies* by Susan Wald and the Language Experts at Berlitz (Wiley Publishing).

After the brief review of the verb tense and a few pertinent examples, each chapter follows up with practice opportunities to reinforce what you discovered.

Foolish Assumptions

When writing this book, I made the following foolish assumptions about you:

- ✔ You already have a background in Spanish, have learned all of the verb tenses, and are looking for an opportunity to review and practice that knowledge. If you're a rank beginner, *Spanish For Dummies* is a great place to start.

- ✔ You've taken at least two years of Spanish or the equivalent.

- ✔ You're boning up on Spanish verbs for your own edification or your son, daughter, grandson, granddaughter, niece, nephew, or special someone is taking their second or third year of Spanish, and you want to help, but you haven't looked at a verb conjugation for years.

- ✔ You love Spanish (like me!), and you actually enjoy conjugating verbs. . . . Okay, so that may be pushing it just a little.

How This Book is Organized

All books in the *For Dummies* series are divided into parts so that you can zero in on your topic of preference and quickly skip anything that looks boring or inconsequential. The chapters in *Spanish Verbs For Dummies* fall into the following seven parts.

Unlike most other Spanish verb books on the market, which group lessons according to tense, *Spanish Verbs For Dummies* starts with the easier verb forms and progresses to the more complex. I think this approach makes the topic a little less intimidating and much more accessible for most beginning learners, but feel free to skip around. Use the following part descriptions as your road map.

Part 1: Presenting the Present Tense

The present is the culmination of the past and the springboard to the future, making it the perfect place to begin any discussion of Spanish verbs. This part introduces Spanish verbs, provides plenty of practice with regular verbs in the present tense, shows you how to phrase commands and questions, and then leaves you coming and going with the verbs **venir** and **ir.** In this part, I promise not to dig up anything from the past or mention concerns about the future.

Part II: Exploring Some Exceptional Exceptions

Every language rule has its exceptions, and the rules covering Spanish verbs are no exceptions. The chapters in this part help you deal with Spanish verbs that don't know how to behave. You figure out how to express your likes and dislikes with the verb **gustar,** differentiate between being and *being* with the verbs **ser** and **estar,** cope with the peculiarities of stem-changing and spelling-changing verbs, and deal with a handful of other Spanish verb oddities.

Part III: Working Out with the Remaining Simple Tenses

Although everyone lives in the present, you constantly look back at the past and forward to the future, so you need a way to describe actions that happen at different times. The chapters in this part show you how to form the six remaining simple tenses: preterit, imperfect, future, conditional, subjunctive (mood), and imperfect subjunctive. This part focuses on regular verbs, so you don't have to worry about the nasty exceptions. Those are covered in Part IV.

Part IV: Coping with Irregular Verbs

Mastering the rules and regulations that govern the conjugation of Spanish verbs can take you only so far. Eventually, you need to find out how to conjugate the irregular verbs — the verbs that break the rules. The chapters in this part show you how to conjugate the most common irregular verbs in the seven simple tenses and provide plenty of practice activities to help tattoo the conjugation charts onto your gray matter.

Part V: Getting Help with the Helping Verb Haber

When it comes to Spanish verbs, even Spanish verbs can use a little help. Through the use of the verb **haber** you can transform the seven simple tenses into seven compound tenses to describe actions that generally happened *before* other actions. Sound confusing? Well, you're right; it's confusing. But the chapters in this part make the concept crystal clear and provide hands-on examples and exercises that can make it seem like second nature.

Part VI: Part of Tens

No *For Dummies* book would be complete without a Part of Tens to provide you with some quick tips and a couple handfuls of useful tidbits you can immediately put to good use. *Spanish Verbs for Dummies* provides three chapters of 10 items each — 30 in all! Here you pick up 10 Spanish idioms, 10 verbs for holidays and other special occasions, and the 10 most frequently asked questions in Spanish (and their replies). I was going to include 10 Spanish curses, but my editor censored the chapter.

Part VII: Appendixes

Throughout this book, you may come across exercises that include some unfamiliar words, so I stuck a few appendixes at the back of the book for quick reference. As you can quickly see by scanning them, they are in no way intended as comprehensive references. If you want a thorough reference, you can purchase any of several Spanish dictionaries or specialized Spanish verb references. I included a brief English/Spanish and Spanish/English glossary to help you with the vocabulary that you may not know and a list of common irregular verb conjugations.

Icons Used in This Book

Every *For Dummies* book has a generous collection of notes, tips, warnings, and other essential and entertaining insights spattered across its pages, and this book is no different. To prevent you from inadvertently overlooking some particularly valuable piece of advice, I flagged each of these golden nuggets of knowledge with one of the following icons.

Example icons pop up wherever it's best for me to *show* you, rather than *tell* you how to form or use a particular verb conjugation. Before you begin an exercise, check out the Example icons to see how it's done.

Tip icons appear to cue you in on a time-saving suggestion or shortcut. If I know an easier way to perform a particular task or remember a tough-to-grasp concept or conjugation, I share it with you by way of these tips.

Remember icons are there to poke you in the ribs so you make sure to commit to memory an important tidbit of information. The points marked with these icons can usually make your life a little easier.

Practice icons flag the beginning of a practice exercise. In some cases, you may want to skip ahead to the practice exercise to test your knowledge *before* you read my explanation of it. If you can complete the exercise correctly on your own, you may not need the brief refresher course. If you get fewer than eight out of ten answers correct, though, you may need to review.

Where to Go from Here

So much for the preliminaries. Now it's time to dive right in to the sea of Spanish verbs and immerse yourself in its 14 tenses and a never-ending stream of conjugation charts, rules, and exceptions.

The most important advice I can give you before you start your journey is to take a fearless, confident approach when checking out any topic, especially a second or third or fourth language. You didn't learn your first language without making countless mistakes, and you certainly won't learn your next language without a few trips and stumbles. The only people who don't make it are the students who quit. Stick with it, make bold mistakes, and if you're committed to communicating with someone in Spanish, you'll eventually get it.

And don't forget — if you haven't already read *Spanish For Dummies,* be sure to pick up a copy and start practicing some conversational Spanish. *Spanish For Dummies* shows you the bare-bones basics and then provides chapter after chapter showing you how to use your Spanish in the real Spanish-speaking world.

Part I

Presenting the Present Tense

The 5th Wave   By Rich Tennant

"Honey, can you look in the phrase book and tell me how 'scrambled' is pronounced in Spanish?"

In this part . . .

The present is a pivotal point — the culmination of the past and the springboard to the future. As such, the present is a good place to start when studying verbs in any language and a great place to begin brushing up on the basics.

In this part, I introduce you to Spanish verbs, the subject pronouns that commonly accompany them, and the four main verb types. You get to warm up with some regular verbs in the present tense, modify actions with adverbs, build sentences, and figure out how to speak in the passive voice (for those rare occasions when you want to remove yourself from what you have to say). You also encounter some special constructions including commands, yes/no questions, and interrogatives.

Chapter 1

Springing into Action with Spanish Verbs

*B*efore you immerse yourself in any heavy-duty verb conjugations, take some time to brush up on the basics so you can effectively communicate using the various verb types. You need to understand

- ✓ What a verb is
- ✓ What the basic verb types are
- ✓ What sorts of subject pronouns you can use to describe the being performing the action
- ✓ What a conjugation chart is

This chapter eases you into the subject of Spanish verbs by defining verbs and showing you how to classify them. You discover how to identify the parts of a verb, the subject pronouns that identify the person or thing performing the action, and the four different types of verbs you may meet on the street. The exercises in this chapter give you a solid framework on which to build your newfound skills.

Recognizing the Four Main Verb Types

Spanish verbs hang out in their own cliques, and each group has its own way of doing things. If you're going to have any success dealing with Spanish verbs, you'd better be able to identify which of the four following groups a verb belongs to:

- ✓ **Regular verbs:** These verbs are easy to get along with because they follow the regular conjugation rules for **-ar, -er,** and **-ir** verbs. You'll like these guys (see the next section and Chapter 2).

- ✓ **Stem-changing verbs:** These verbs morph depending on how you use them in a sentence. You'll encounter three types of stem-changing verbs, classified according to their stem changes: *e* to *i*, *e* to *ie*, and *o* to *ue* (see Chapter 8).

- ✓ **Spelling-change verbs:** Consonant spelling changes occur in some of the conjugated forms of these verbs. The changes enable the verbs to comply with pronunciation rules of the particular letters. The affected consonants are *c*, *g*, and *z* (see Chapter 8)

✔ **Reflexive verbs:** Whenever you do something to yourself, you use a reflexive verb to express the fact that the action is performed or "reflected back" on you, the subject of the sentence. Reflexive verbs are accompanied by reflexive pronouns, like *herself* or *themselves;* for example, "Barry poked *himself* in the eye." The reflexive pronoun has to agree with the subject of the sentence and follow the placement rules for all *object pronouns,* the pronouns that receive the action (see Chapter 3).

Getting the Lowdown on Regular Spanish Verbs

Verbs are action words. They're the movers and the shakers of the world. They describe the action that is taking place, has taken place, or will take place. They command, they question, they conjecture, and they describe states of being. No sentence is complete without one.

A raw verb is expressed as an *infinitive.* In English, that means the *to* form — "to eat," for example. Nobody's doing the eating, and the eating is not being done at any specific time or in any specific way, and nobody's really eating anything. An infinitive is an action, pure and simple.

In Spanish, you have no *to* to rely on. Spanish expresses the infinitive form of its verbs through verb endings: **-ar, -er,** and **-ir.** For example, **hablar** (to speak), **comer** (to eat), and **vivir** (to live). All Spanish verbs use one of these three endings. When you chop off the **-ar, -er,** or **-ir** endings, the remaining letters make up the *verb stem.*

Below are some regular Spanish verbs. Determine each verb's stem and classify it as an **-ar, -er,** or **-ir** verb, as I show you in the following example:

hablar = *habl, - ar*

1. vivir = _____ , - _____

2. comer = _____ , - _____

3. abrir = _____ , - _____

4. presentar = _____ , - _____

5. mirar = _____ , - _____

6. astar = _____ , - _____

7. escribir = _____ , - _____

8. leer = _____ , - _____

9. romper = _____ , - _____

10. suprimir = _____ , - _____

Meeting Subject Pronouns Face to Face

I, we, you, he, she, it, and *they* are the English subject pronouns. They tell the verb who or what is performing the action, and they dictate the form of the verb you must use. In English, he *shops,* but they *shop.*

Spanish uses nine subject pronouns: **(yo, tú, usted, él, ella, nosotros** or **nosotras, vosotros** or **vosotras, ustedes,** and **ellos** or **ellas).** The subject pronoun determines the conjugated form of the verb. Just like in English, the Spanish infinitive form of the verb means that no one is doing the action, but the conjugated form signifies that some individual or group is performing the action. Whenever you conjugate a verb, you set up a chart, like the one that follows, and fill in each subject pronoun's accompanying verb form.

Spanish Subject Pronouns	
yo = I **nosotras** = we (female group)	**nosotros** = we (mixed or male group)
tú = you (familiar) **vosotras** = you (familiar, female group)	**vosotros** you (familiar, mixed or male group)
él = he **ella** = she **usted (Ud.)** = you (formal)	**ellos** = they (mixed or male group) **ellas** = female group **ustedes (Uds.)** you (formal)

Although **usted** is usually abbreviated to **Ud.** when written, you still pronounce it **usted.** Likewise, although **ustedes** is usually abbreviated to **Uds.** when written, you still pronounce it **ustedes.**

The **vosotros** form (*you* plural, familiar) is used almost exclusively in Spain. In its place, other countries use the **Uds.** form of the verb. Also, keep in mind that in English, only one *you* is used for all four of the Spanish *you's* (although sometimes for the plural *you,* you may say "you guys" if you're from the North or "y'all" if you're from the South — so in that way English-speakers sort of create a plural *you).*

Select the correct Spanish subject pronoun to replace the following names or nouns. (Unless specified, the familiar *you* is the singular form.) Here's an example:

Jim = *él*

11. my friends (mixed or male group) = _____

12. the students (mixed or male group) = _____

13. she = _____

14. you (familiar) = _____

15. my parents = _____

16. my best friend (male) = _____

17. Bob and Tom = _____

18. her dad = _____

19. Susan = _____

20. George and I = _____

Answer Key

Below are some regular Spanish verbs. Determine each verb's stem and classify it as an **-ar**, **-er**, or **-ir** verb.

1. vivir = *viv, - ir*

2. comer = *com, - er*

3. abrir = *abr, - ir*

4. presentar = *present, - ar*

5. mirar = *mir, - ar*

6. gastar = *gast, - ar*

7. escribir = *escrib, - ir*

8. leer = *le, - er*

9. romper = *romp, - er*

10. suprimir = *suprim, - ir*

Select the correct Spanish subject pronoun to replace the following names or nouns. (Unless specified, the familiar *you* is the singular form.)

11. my friends (mixed or male group) = *ellos*

12. the students (mixed or male group) = *ellos*

13. she = *ella*

14. you (familiar) = *tú*

15. my parents = *ellos*

16. my best friend (male) = *él*

17. Bob and Tom = *ellos*

18. her dad = *él*

19. Susan = *ella*

20. George and I = *nosotros*

Chapter 2

Warming Up with Regular Verbs in the Present Tense

In This Chapter

▶ Loosening up with present tense **-ar, -er,** and **-ir** verb conjugations

▶ Speaking in complete sentences

▶ Adding character to your verbs with adverbs

▶ Discovering the personal **a** and the passive voice

Most verbs are fairly well-behaved. They follow the rules. They're predictable, especially in the present tense, which makes them fairly easy to master. The regular Spanish verbs come in three flavors — **-ar, -er,** and **-ir** — and you won't find anything tricky about conjugating them. Regular verbs, therefore, are a great place to start your warm-up exercises with the present tense.

In this chapter, you work exclusively with the three regular verb forms in the present tense. You find out how to conjugate all three using the subject pronoun chart I introduce in Chapter 1 — no exceptions, I promise. This chapter also provides a list of commonly used regular **-ar, -er,** and **-ir** verbs, so you can get in some additional practice on your own.

To keep you from dozing off with the easy stuff, I've thrown in some adverbs so you can tell people when particular actions or events are occurring. You also discover how to

✔ Build a sentence in Spanish, complete with subject and verb

✔ Use the personal **a**

✔ Avoid taking responsibility for your actions by using the passive voice — an essential lesson for all budding politicians

Conjugating -ar Verbs

Conjugating regular **-ar** verbs is a snap. You take the infinitive form of the verb, which ends in **-ar,** chop off the **-ar,** and replace it with the ending for the appropriate subject pronouns: *I, you, he, she, we,* or *they.* If you need to review subject pronouns and how they influence verb conjugations, refer to Chapter 1. I'm going to present all verb conjugations in these three-row, two-column boxes until you're sick and tired of seeing them, so master the concept of subject pronouns before you go any further.

The subject pronoun dictates the verb form that you use in a sentence. If you start a sentence with *I,* for example, and you use an **-ar** verb, that verb must end in **-o.**

Regular present tense -ar verb endings:

yo -o	nosotros/as -amos
tú -as	vosotros/as -áis
él, ella -a Ud.	ellos/as -an Uds.

So the present-tense conjugations for a regular **-ar** verb such as **hablar** (to speak) are . . .

hablar = to speak	
hablo	hablamos
hablas	habláis
habla	hablan
Yo **hablo** español. = I *speak* Spanish.	

Now I bet you want a few more **-ar** verbs to play with, so Table 2-1 shows some commonly used regular **-ar** verbs that you can throw around at your next dinner party.

Table 2-1	Common Regular *-ar* Verbs
Term	*Translation*
andar	to walk
anunciar	to announce
arreglar	to fix
ayudar	to help
bailar	to dance
caminar	to walk
cantar	to sing
celebrar	to celebrate
cenar	to eat supper
cepillar	to brush
charlar	to chat
cocinar	to cook
comprar	to buy
cortar	to cut
dibujar	to draw
escuchar	to listen (to)
estudiar	to study
ganar	to win, to earn
lavar	to wash
limpiar	to clean
mirar	to look (at)

Unlike in English, which keeps its verbs and prepositions separate, some verbs in the Spanish language include a preposition (like *to* or *at*). Table 2-1 includes two such verbs: **escuchar** and **mirar.** As a native English speaker, you may be tempted to toss in an extra preposition. Avoid the temptation.

Translate the following subjects and verbs into Spanish. The subject pronoun guides you in selecting the correct conjugation, and the verb must agree with the subject. In some cases when you follow a subject with a conjugated verb, you create a simple sentence. For details about creating sentences, refer to "Building a Sentence from the Ground Up" later in this chapter.

The **vosotros** form isn't used in this activity, so when you see *you (plural)* use the **Uds.** form.

Here's an example, to get you started:

we celebrate = *nosotros celebramos*

1. I clean = _____

2. you (familiar, singular) sing = _____

3. we help = _____

4. they (female) wash = _____

5. you (plural, formal) watch = _____

6. he cuts = _____

7. she dances = _____

8. I walk = _____

9. you (singular, formal) brush = _____

10. we chat = _____

11. they clean = _____

12. he eats supper = _____

13. she walks = _____

14. I fix = _____

15. you (familiar) celebrate = _____

16. she draws = _____

17. he wins = _____

18. we buy = _____

19. they (female) cut = _____

20. you (plural, formal) study = _____

Conjugating -er Verbs

The **-ar** verbs set the pattern for all the regular verbs, including the **-er** and **-ir** verbs. To conjugate **-er** verbs, you chop the **-er** off the end of the verb and add the appropriate verb endings so that the verb agrees with its subject pronoun. If you can etch the following conjugation chart on your gray matter, you'll have everything you need to conjugate any **-er** verb you may encounter.

Regular present tense -er verb endings:

yo -o	nosotros/as -emos
tú -es	vosotros/as -éis
él, ella -e Ud.	ellos/as -en Uds.

So the present-tense conjugations for a regular **-er** verb such as **aprender** (to understand) are . . .

aprender = to understand	
aprendo	aprendemos
aprendes	aprendéis
aprende	aprenden
Nosotros **aprendemos.** = We *understand.*	

Understanding is certainly necessary, but you don't want to restrict all of your actions to such a passive activity, so Table 2-2 gives you some additional **-er** verbs that are a little more fun and interesting.

Table 2-2	Commmon Regular *-er* Verbs
Term	*Translation*
aprender	to learn
barrer	to sweep
beber	to drink
comer	to eat
comprender	to understand
corer	to run
creer	to believe
deber	to owe, must, ought
depender	to depend

Term	Translation
leer	to read
poseer	to possess, own
responder	to respond
romper	to break
socorrer	to help
sorprender	to surprise
tañer	to pluck, to play a stringed musical instrument
temer	to fear, dread
vender	to sell

Translate the following subjects and verbs into Spanish, as I show you here:

you (familiar) respond = *tú respondes*

21. I help = _____

22. you (familiar) understand = _____

23. he learns = _____

24. she should = _____

25. they respond = _____

26. we dread = _____

27. you (plural, formal) eat = _____

28. I depend = _____

29. she runs = _____

30. he possesses = _____

31. we drink = _____

32. they (female) read = _____

33. I sweep = _____

34. you (plural, formal) believe = _____

35. you (singular, familiar) play a stringed instrument= _____

Conjugating -ir Verbs

The **-ar** and **-er** verbs make up the bulk of the regular verbs, but a small number of **-ir** verbs round out the collection. You conjugate these verbs the same as the **-er** verbs, except for the **nosotros** and the **vosotros** forms. The following conjugation chart shows just what I mean.

Regular present tense -ir verb endings:

yo -o	nosotros/as -imos
tú -es	vosotros/as -ís
él, ella -e Ud.	ellos/as -en Uds.

The present tense conjugations for a regular **-ir** verb such as **escribir** (to write) are . . .

escribir = to write	
escribo	escribimos
escribes	escribís
escribe	escriben
Ella **escribe.** = She *writes*.	

Although the collection of regular **-ir** verbs is relatively small, it includes a respectable number of verbs that you simply can't live without. Here, in Table 2-3, are some commonly used regular **-ir** verbs to give you some additional examples to work with.

Table 2-3	Common Regular *-ir* Verbs
Term	*Translation*
abrir	to open
aburrir	to annoy, to bore
admitir	to admit
añadir	to add
aplaudir	to applaud
assistir	to attend
cubrir	to cover
cumplir cumplir ___ años	to fulfill to complete ___ years
decidir	to decided
describir	to describe
descubrir	to discover
discutir	to discuss, to debate

Term	Translation
imprimir	to impress, to imprint
inscriber	to inscribe, to record
permitir	to permit
prohibir	to prohibit
recibir	to receive
repartir	to distribute, to deal cards

Translate the following subjects and verbs into Spanish. Here's an example to get you started:

they (female) = *ellas permiten*

36. they cover = _____

37. he discovers = _____

38. I prohibit = _____

39. you (familiar) receive = _____

40. she records = _____

41. you (plural, formal) decide = _____

42. we imprint = _____

43. I open = _____

44. they applaud = _____

45. she attends = _____

46. he bores = _____

47. you (plural, formal) admit = _____

48. we discuss = _____

49. she permits = _____

50. you (singular, familiar) deal cards = _____

Timing Your Actions with Adverbs

The tense is built right into the verb, but that isn't always specific enough to describe precisely when an action is occurring in the present. Is it happening now, sometimes, always, every Saturday? By tacking on an adverb, you can express time more precisely.

The present tense in Spanish conveys not only an ongoing present tense action, such as "I'm talking on the phone," but also an action that you're in the habit of doing, such as "I talk on the phone a lot." Adverbs help you make those distinctions.

Table 2-4 gives a list of adverbs commonly used with the present tense:

Table 2-4	Present-Tense Adverbs
Term	*Translation*
a veces	sometimes
ahora	now
ahora mismo	right now
con frecuencia	often
nunca	never
mucho	a lot
siempre	always
todos los días	every day
todos los meses	every month
todos los años	every year
todo el tiempo	all of the time
todos los sábados	every Saturday

Building a Sentence from the Ground Up

A subject and a verb are all you really need to create a bona fide sentence: **Yo canto** (I sing). That's a sentence. In Spanish, you can even drop the subject when its meaning is understood from the verb ending: **Canto.** Now that's one short sentence.

Of course, if you walk around Spain or Mexico or some other Spanish-speaking country expressing yourself in one-word sentences, you'll come across as being a little odd. Most of the time, you want to convey a little (or a lot) more information. You want to indicate when something happened, why it happened, who was performing the action, and what the action was being performed on.

When you have more to say, you can turn to some other parts of speech, such as the adverbs I discuss in the preceding section. By putting a subject, verb, adverb, and some other select words together, you can begin to express yourself in Spanish.

If you use two verbs together and the second one is in the infinitive form, you don't need anything between them unless they're a part of a *verb structure,* a commonly used phrase that contains one or more verbs. For information about them, check out Chapter 3.

Translate the following sentences into Spanish. Included are **-ar, -er,** and **-ir** verbs, and the adverbs that I list in the preceding section. Unless otherwise specified, the *you* subject is the familiar **tú.** If you encounter any unfamiliar words or expressions, you can look up their meanings in the English-Spanish glossary at the end of the book.

51. I help in the house every week.

_____

52. They are dancing at the party.

_____

53. You (plural, formal) ought to study every day.

_____

54. He understands English and Spanish.

_____

55. I run in the park every Saturday.

_____

56. We are watching TV in the living room.

_____

57. She is describing the photo to the class.

_____

58. They prohibit speaking (to speak) English at home.

_____

59. He is dealing cards at Las Vegas.

_____

60. We clean the house a lot.

_____

61. I sweep the floor every day.

_____

62. We open the door when we should.

_____

63. You (plural, formal) always dance at parties.

_____

64. The students respond when the teacher announces the problem.

_____

65. They discuss very important things in history class.

_____

66. My parents attend the concerts at the school when I sing.

_____

67. I walk in the park every Sunday.

_____

68. She washes the dishes after dinner every day.

_____

69. Young people listen to music a lot.

_____

70. We read many novels in the summer.

_____

Getting Chummy with the Personal "a"

In Spanish, the preposition *to* is **a.** If you want to say "to the store," for example, you say "**a la tienda.**"

Spanish has a very important use for **a** that doesn't even translate to English, and that's the personal **a.** Whenever the direct object of the verb is a person or a pet, the direct object *must* be preceded by the Spanish personal **a.**

This rule is sometimes hard to remember because it has no English equivalent, but a few examples can help drive home the point:

Ellos ayudan a los estudiantes mucho.	= They help the students a lot.
Los estudiantes escuchan a la profesora.	= The students listen to the teacher.
Yo ayudo a mi mamá en la cocina todos los días.	= I help my mom in the kitchen every day.
Él escucha la radio.	= He listens to the radio. (Because the verb **escuchar** includes the preposition, in the English translation *to listen to,* you omit the preposition before *the radio.*)

Translate the following statements into Spanish. Some include the personal **a,** and some don't. Here's an example:

Él camina a su perro en el parque todas las tardes. = *He walks his dog in the park every afternoon.*

71. The students understand the teacher when she speaks Spanish.

_____

72. They always help their parents at home on the weekend.

_____

73. She sings at school every day.

_____

74. He opens the door for the girls.

_____

75. I wash my dog every week.

_____

76. We walk with our friends in the park every Saturday.

_____

77. I surprise my parents when I wash the dishes and clean the house.

_____

78. They walk their dog a lot.

_____

79. The teacher bores the students when he talks too much.

_____

80. She is describing her boyfriend to her family right now.

_____

Speaking of the Passive Voice . . .

When you want a lesson in using the passive voice, tune into a Washington press conference. During the press conference, you rarely hear about the person or persons responsible for making a particular decision or performing a specific action. Instead, you hear passive constructions like these:

- ✔ The decision *was made* last July.
- ✔ Action *was taken* to stem the violence.
- ✔ Authorities *were called* in to investigate.
- ✔ Funds *were misappropriated.*

With the passive voice, you never know who's performing the action, which sometimes is exactly how you want to present certain information, especially if you're a scientist or a politician. Following are some additional examples:

- ✔ No swimming *is allowed* after 10 p.m.
- ✔ No eating *is allowed* outside of the dining room.
- ✔ English and Spanish *are spoken* here.
- ✔ French *is spoken* in France.

In Spanish, you form the passive voice with **se** and either the third-person singular or the third-person plural of the verb in question. The noun or nouns that follow the conjugated verb determine whether the verb is singular or plural in form. In other words, a singular noun is preceded by a verb in its singular form, and a plural noun or multiple nouns are preceded by a verb in its plural form.

The following list provides translations of the English statements in the preceding bulleted list:

- ✔ **No se permite nadar después de las 10 p.m.**
- ✔ **No se permite comer fuera del comedor.**
- ✔ **Se hablan inglés y español aquí.**
- ✔ **Se habla francés en Francia.**

Answer *C* for *cierto* (true), or *F* for *falso* (false) to the following statements in the passive voice.

81. _____ Se debe practicar el español todos los días.

82. _____ Se sirven muchas hamburguesas en McDonald's.

83. _____ Se debe nadar pronto después de comer mucho.

84. _____ Se habla inglés en Inglaterra.

85. _____ Se habla alemán en España.

86. _____ Normalmente, se sirve mucha champaña en una boda.

87. _____ Se permite fumar en los aviones.

88. _____ Se debe poner un traje de baño cuando hace mucho frío.

89. _____ Se necesita estudiar antes de un examen importante.

90. _____ Se debe ir a la biblioteca para encontrar un libro.

Answer Key

Translate the following subjects and verbs into Spanish. Let the subject pronoun guide you in selecting the correct conjugation; the verb must agree with the subject.

1. I clean = *yo limpio*

2. you (familiar) sing = *tú cantas*

3. we help = *nosotros ayudamos*

4. they (female) wash = *ellas lavan*

5. you (plural, formal) watch = *Uds. miran*

6. he cuts = *él corta*

7. she dances = *ella baila*

8. I walk = *yo camino*

9. you (formal) brush = *Ud. cepilla*

10. we chat = *nosotros charlamos*

11. they clean = *ellos limpian*

12. he eats supper = *él cena*

13. she walks = *ella anda*

14. I fix = *yo arreglo*

15. you (familiar) celebrate = *tú celebras*

16. she draws = *ella dibuja*

17. he wins = *él gana*

18. we buy = *nosotros compramos*

19. they (female) cut = *ellas cortan*

20. you (plural, formal) study = *Uds. estudian*

Translate the following subjects and verbs into Spanish.

21. I help = *yo socorro*

22. you (familiar) understand = *tú comprendes*

23. he learns = *él aprende*

24. she should = *ella debe*

25. they respond = *ellos responden*

26. we dread = *nosotros tememos*

27. you (plural, formal) eat = *Uds. comen*

28. I depend = *yo dependo*

29. she runs = *ella corre*

30. he possesses = *él posee*

31. we drink = *nosotros bebemos*

32. they (female) read = *ellas leen*

33. I sweep = *yo barro*

34. you (plural, formal) believe = *Uds. creen*

35. you (familiar) play a stringed instrument = *tú tañes*

Translate the following subjects and verbs into Spanish.

36. they cover = *ellos cubren*

37. he discovers = *él descubre*

38. I prohibit = *yo prohibo*

39. you (familiar) receive = *tú recibes*

40. she records = *ella inscribe*

41. you (plural, formal) decide = *Uds. deciden*

42. we imprint = *nosotros imprimimos*

43. I open = *yo abro*

44. they applaud = *ellos aplauden*

45. she attends = *ella asiste*

46. he bores = *él aburre*

47. you (plural, formal) admit = *Uds. admiten*

48. we discuss = *nosotros discutimos*

49. she permits = *ella permite*

50. you (familiar) deal cards = *tú repartes*

Translate the following sentences into Spanish. Included are **-ar, -er,** and **-ir** verbs, and the adverbs that are listed in the previous section. Unless otherwise specified, the *you* subject is **tú.**

51. I help in the house every week.

Yo ayudo en la casa cada semana.

52. They are dancing at the party.

Ellos bailan en la fiesta.

53. You (plural, formal) ought to study every day.

Uds. deben estudiar todos los días.

54. He understands English and Spanish.

Él comprende inglés y español.

55. I run in the park every Saturday.

Yo corro en el parque todos los sábados.

56. We are watching T.V. in the living room.

Nosotros miramos la televisión en la sala.

57. She is describing the photo to the class.

Ella describe la foto a la clase.

58. They prohibit speaking (to speak) English at home.

Ellos prohiben hablar inglés en casa.

59. He is dealing cards at Las Vegas.

Él reparte los naipes en Las Vegas.

60. We clean the house a lot.

Nosotros limpiamos la casa mucho.

61. I sweep the floor everyday.

Yo barro el suelo todos los días.

62. We open the door when we should.

Nosotros abrimos la puerta cuando debemos.

63. You (plural, formal) always dance at parties.

Uds. siempre bailan en las fiestas.

64. The students respond when the teacher announces the problem.

Los estudiantes responden cuando la profesora anuncia el problema.

65. They discuss very important things in history class.

Ellos discuten cosas muy importantes en la clase de historia.

66. My parents attend the concerts at the school when I sing.

Mis padres asisten a los conciertos en la escuela cuando yo canto.

67. I walk in the park every Sunday.

Yo camino en el parque todos los domingos.

68. She washes the dishes after dinner every day.

Ella lava los platos después de la cena todos los días.

69. Young people listen to music a lot.

Los jóvenes escuchan la música mucho.

70. We read many novels in the summer.

Nosotros leemos muchas novelas en el verano.

Translate the following statements into Spanish. Some will include the personal **a,** and some won't.

71. The students understand the teacher when she speaks Spanish.

Los estudiantes comprenden a la profesora cuando ella habla español.

72. They always help their parents at home on the week-end.

Ellos siempre ayudan a sus padres en la casa los fines de semana.

73. She sings at school every day.

Ella canta en la escuela todos los días.

74. He opens the door for the girls.

Él abre la puerta para las muchachas.

75. I wash my dog every week.

Yo lavo a mi perro cada semana.

76. We walk with our friends in the park every Saturday.

Nosotros caminamos con nuestros amigos en el parque todos los sábados.

77. I surprise my parents when I wash the dishes and clean the house.

Yo sorprendo a mis padres cuando yo lavo los platos y limpio la casa.

78. They walk their dog a lot.

Ellos caminan a su perro mucho.

79. The teacher bores the students when he talks too much.

El profesor aburre a los estudiantes cuando él habla demasiado.

80. She is describing her boyfriend to her family right now.

Ella describe a su novio a su familia ahora.

Answer *C* for *cierto* (true), or *F* for *falso* (false) to the following statements in the passive voice.

81. *C* Se deber practicar el español todos los días. *(Spanish should be practiced every day.)*

82. *C* Se sirven muchas hamburguesas en McDonald's. *(Many hamburgers are served at McDonald's.)*

83. *F* Se debe nadar pronto después de comer mucho. *(Swimming after eating a lot of food should be done.)*

84. *C* Se habla inglés en Inglaterra. *(English is spoken in England.)*

85. *F* Se habla alemán en España. *(German is spoken in Spain.)*

86. *C* Normalmente, se sirve mucha champaña en una boda. *(Normally, champagine is served at a wedding.)*

87. *F* Se permite fumar en los aviones. *(Smoking is not permitted in planes.)*

88. *F* Se debe poner un traje de baño cuando hace mucho frío. *(A swimsuit should be worn when it's very cold.)*

89. *C* Se necesita estudiar antes de un examen importante. *(Studying should be done before an important exam.)*

90. *C* Se debe ir a la biblioteca para encontrar un libro. *(The library should be visited when you want to find a book.)*

Chapter 3

Constructing Commands and Other Verb Structures

To order someone to carry out a task, you use the *imperative mood*. To express continuing action in the present, you use the *present progressive tense*. To express an action that acts upon the subject of the sentence, you use a *reflexive verb*. In Spanish, you can build these and various other verb structures, and you can use the irregular verb **tener** (to have) to say not only what you *have*, but what you *have to do* and what you *feel like* doing.

In this chapter, you find out how to form these common verb structures, and you get a feel for some of their nuances. After successfully completing the exercises in this chapter, you'll have the confidence and know-how you need to use these verb structures competently in writing and in your next conversation.

Taking Command with the Imperative Mood

When you tell a waiter to bring you water, ask a dinner guest to please pass the salt, or tell your dog to lie down, you're using the *imperative mood*. You're giving a command — telling someone, or sometimes yourself, to do something.

The imperative is called a *mood*, rather than a *tense*, because it deals with wants and desires, and the time is always *now*.

In most cases, you bark out commands in the *you* form, but remember that in Spanish *you* can mean any of four different *you's*. With the imperative, you can also give what is called a *Let's* command, as in, "Let's go to the movie." This less assertive form of the imperative takes the **nosotros** form. For more about the four Spanish forms of *you* and other subject pronouns, see Chapter 1.

You can form positive **tú** commands by dropping the **-s** from the present tense **tú** forms of regular **-ar, -er,** or **-ir** verbs:

hablas (you speak) becomes **habla** (speak)

comes (you eat) becomes **come** (eat)

escribes (you write) becomes **escribe** (write)

In Spanish exclamations and questions, the punctuation comes upside down at the beginning of the phrase, as well as at the end.

You can form negative **tú** commands by taking the **-o** off of the present-tense **yo** form and adding **-es** for regular **-ar** verbs and **-as** for regular **-er** and **-ir** verbs:

> **hablo** (I speak) becomes **no hables** (don't speak)
>
> **como** (I eat) becomes **no comas** (don't eat)
>
> **escribo** (I write) becomes **no escribas** (don't write)

Spanish also includes some irregular **tú** form commands. Table 3-1 shows the positive and negative forms of the most common irregular **tú** form commands:

Table 3-1	Irregular Tú Form Commands	
Infinitive	*Positive Command*	*Negative Command*
decir = to say, tell	**di**	**no digas**
hacer = to do, make	**haz**	**no hagas**
ir = to go	**ve**	**no vayas**
poner = to put	**pon**	**no pongas**
salir = to leave	**sal**	**no salgas**
ser = to be	**sé**	**no seas**
tener = to have	**ten**	**no tengas**
venir = to come	**ven**	**no vengas**

Write the following **tú** form commands in Spanish, as I show you here:

Speak Spanish. = *Habla español.*

1. Open the window.

   _____

2. Sing.

   _____

3. Don't watch TV.

   _____

4. Leave.

   _____

5. Don't be foolish!

   _____

6. Dance.

   _____

7. Listen to the teacher.

   _____

8. Deal the cards.

   _____

9. Don't bore the students.

   _____

10. Don't leave late.

    _____

11. Wash the dishes.

    _____

12. Clean the house.

    _____

13. Run.

    _____

14. Walk.

    _____

15. Talk louder.

    _____

16. Study for the exam.

    _____

17. Describe your house.

    _____

18. Do not attend the concert.

    _____

19. Do not surprise the children.

    _____

20. Read the newspaper every day.

    _____

21. Put the book on the table.

    _____

22. Celebrate!

_____

23. Don't come early.

_____

24. Don't do the homework today.

_____

25. Don't break the dishes!

_____

Forming the formal "you" singular command

When forming the formal *you* singular, or the **usted (Ud.)** commands in the positive and the negative forms, you drop the **-o** ending of the **yo** form, and add an **-e** for **-ar** verbs or an **-a** for **-er** and **-ir** verbs. Here are a few examples:

Hable. = Speak.	**No hable.** = Don't speak.
Coma. =Eat.	**No coma.** =Don't eat.
Escriba. = Write.	**No escriba.** = Don't write.

Spanish has only the following three irregular **usted** commands:

Infinitive	*Positive Command*	*Negative Command*
ir	**Vaya.** = Go.	**No vaya.** = Don't go.
saber	**Sepa.** = Know.	**No sepa.** = Don't know.
ser	**Sea.** = Be.	**No sea.** = Don't be.

Write the following **Ud.** commands in Spanish. Here's an example:

Speak Spanish. = *Hable español.*

26. Play the piano.

_____

27. Don't sing this song.

_____

28. Walk to the store.

_____

29. Run fast.

_____

30. Don't study all the time.

_____

31. Don't eat dinner now.

_____

32. Help the students.

_____

33. Don't eat before dinner.

_____

34. Prepare the lesson.

_____

35. Wash the dishes.

_____

Forming the formal "you" plural command

When forming the formal, plural *you* or **ustedes (Uds.)** commands, you simply add an **-n** to the Ud. command form. This rule applies for the regular and irregular verbs, as shown in the following examples:

> **Hablen.** = Speak.
>
> **¡No coman!** = Don't eat!
>
> **Escriban.** = Write.
>
> **¡No sean tontos!** = Don't be foolish!

Write the following **Uds.** commands in Spanish, as in the following example:

Open your books. = *Abran sus libros.*

36. Go to bed.

_____

37. Be good.

_____

38. Clean your rooms.

_____

39. Help the teacher.

_____

40. Don't run in the school.

_____

41. Eat the dinner.

_____

42. Cut the paper.

_____

43. Read the story.

_____

44. Sing louder.

_____

45. Talk to the manager.

_____

Forming the informal "you" plural command

When forming the positive, informal, plural _you_ or **vosotros** commands for regular verbs, you drop the **-r** from the infinitive form and add **-d,** as you can see in the following examples:

> **¡Hablad!** = Speak!
>
> **Comed.** = Eat.
>
> **Escribid.** = Write.

When forming the negative **vosotros** commands, you simply drop the **-o** from the present-tense **yo** form and add **-éis** for **-ar** verbs or **-áis** for **-er** and **-ir** verbs, as follows:

> **¡No habléis!** = Don't speak!
>
> **No comáis.** = Don't eat.
>
> **No escribáis.** = Don't write.

The same three verbs are irregular in the negative **vosotros** command forms as in the **usted** forms. They are

Infinitive	_Negative Command_	_Translation_
ir	**¡No vayáis!**	Don't go!
saber	**No sepáis . . .**	Don't know . . .
ser	**No seáis . . .**	Don't be . . .

Write the following **vosotros** form commands in Spanish. Here's an example:

Don't work too much. = *No trabajad demasiado.*

46. Chat with your friends.

_____

47. Don't talk on the phone so much.

_____

48. Go to the store.

_____

49. Don't believe everything that they say.

_____

50. Eat all of your food.

_____

51. Tell the truth.

_____

52. Dance at the party.

_____

53. Sell all of the old books.

_____

54. Don't talk to the other students during the test.

_____

55. Win the game.

_____

Forming the "Let's" command

The **nosotros** form commands, or the *let's* commands, enable you to make suggestions to your friends or to a group of people (including yourself) about what you want to do. When forming these commands, take the **-o** off of the present-tense **yo** form of the verb and add **-emos** for **-ar** verbs or **-amos** for **-er** and **-ir** verbs. You simply put **no** in front of the verb to make a negative *let's* command. Some examples follow in Table 3-2:

Table 3-2	*Let's* Commands with Regular Verbs			
Infinitive (Ending)	**Positive Command**	**Translation**	**Negative Command**	**Translation**
hablar (-ar)	**Hablemos.**	Let's talk.	**No hablemos.**	Let's not talk.
comer (-er)	**Comamos.**	Let's eat.	**No comamos.**	Let's not eat.
escribir (-ir)	**Escribamos.**	Let's write.	**No escribamos.**	Let's not write.

The three verbs in Table 3-3 are irregular in the **vosotros** command form, both in their positive and the negative formations. Note that **-ir** is different in its positive and negative forms.

Table 3-3	*Let's* Commands with Irregular Verbs			
Infinitive (Ending)	**Positive Command**	**Translation**	**Negative Command**	**Translation**
ir	**Vamos.**	Let's go.	**No vayamos.**	Let's not go.
saber	**Sepamos.**	Let's know.	**No sepamos.**	Let's not know.
ser	**Seamos.**	Let's be.	**No seamos.**	Let's not be.

Put the following *Let's* form commands in Spanish, as I show you here:

Let's visit our grandparents. = *Visitemos nuestros abuelos.*

56. Let's write.

_____

57. Let's go to the movie.

_____

58. Let's listen to the radio.

_____

59. Let's walk faster.

_____

60. Let's read to the students.

_____

61. Let's help our parents.

_____

62. Let's dance.

_____

63. Let's buy new books.

_____

64. Let's clean the house later.

_____

65. Let's talk on the phone tomorrow.

_____

66. Let's not break the dishes.

_____

67. Let's walk to the store.

_____

68. Let's not draw in the dictionary.

_____

69. Let's not clean the house today.

_____

70. Let's celebrate this weekend.

_____

Acting in the Now with the Present Progressive

You may think that if you're doing something now, you have only one way of expressing that action in the present tense. But, no, that would be far too easy. You can use the simple present tense to describe a current action or an action that you perform on a regular basis, such as "I wash dishes." But you can also express the same present action as something that's taking place right now by using the *present progressive*.

You form the present progressive by taking the present tense of the verb **estar** (to be) and the present participle or *-ing* form of the action verb. When you put these two together, you have *to be* + *doing*. Whoever or whatever is performing the action determines the form of **estar** — which happens to be irregular in the present tense — that you use. First of all, here are the forms of **estar**:

estar = to be	
estoy	estamos
estás	estáis
está	están
Yo **estoy.** = I *am*.	

The second part of this structure consists of the present participle, or *-ing* form, of the action verb, which you form by dropping the **-ar** off the infinitive form of the verb and then adding **-ando.** For **-er** and **-ir** verbs, you drop the **-er** or **-ir** ending and add **-iendo.** Use the following examples as your guide:

> **hablar** (to speak) becomes **hablando** (speaking)
>
> **comer** (to eat) becomes **comiendo** (eating)
>
> **escribir** (to write) becomes **escribiendo** (writing)

When you put it all together, you get the present progressive:

> **Yo estoy hablando.** = I am talking.
>
> **Él está comiendo.** = He is eating.
>
> **Ellos están escribiendo.** = They are writing.

Of course, every crowd has its exceptions. Table 3-4 lays out many of the most common irregular present participles.

Table 3-4		Common Irregular Present Participles	
Infinitive	*Translation*	*Present Participle*	*Translation*
caer	to fall	**cayendo**	falling
construer	to construct	**construyendo**	constructing
corregir	to correct	**corrigiendo**	correcting
creer	to believe	**creyendo**	believing
decir	to say, to tell	**diciendo**	saying, telling
destruir	to destroy	**destruyendo**	destroying
dormir	to sleep	**durmiendo**	sleeping
ir	to go	**yendo**	going
leer	to read	**leyendo**	reading
mentir	to lie, to tell a falsehood	**mintiendo**	lying
morir	to die	**muriendo**	dying
oír	to hear	**oyendo**	hearing
pedir	to ask for, to request	**pidiendo**	asking for, requesting
poder	to be able	**pudiendo**	being able
reír	to laugh	**riendo**	laughing
repetir	to repeat	**repitiendo**	repeating
seguir	to follow	**siguiendo**	following
sentir	to feel	**sintiendo**	feeling
servir	to serve	**sirviendo**	serving
traer	to bring	**trayendo**	bringing
venir	to come	**viniendo**	coming

Write the following present progressive sentences in Spanish, as I show you here:

The team is practicing. = *El equipo está practicando.*

71. She is buying a new car.

_____

72. They are singing at the concert.

_____

73. We are eating in a French restaurant.

_____

74. Juan is listening to his radio.

_____

75. I am walking my dog in the park.

_____

76. The mechanic is repairing the car.

_____

77. They are reading the newspaper.

_____

78. We are discussing the new verbs.

_____

79. Susana is shopping at the new mall.

_____

80. My mother is preparing dinner.

_____

Reflecting on Reflexive Verbs

Whenever you look at yourself, drive yourself to the mall, or worry yourself silly, you're involved in a reflexive action. You, the subject, are doing something to yourself, the direct object. In English, reflexive actions become a little fuzzy, because so much is considered to be understood. Spanish, however, delineates reflexive action by requiring the use of a reflexive verb and a reflexive pronoun, such as *myself, yourself,* or *herself.*

When creating a reflexive verb construction, you need a subject, a reflexive verb, and a reflexive pronoun, but not necessarily in that order. When you conjugate the reflexive verbs in English, you place the pronouns in front of the conjugated verb. In other words, you say, "You bathe yourself." But in Spanish, the order is *you yourself bathe.*

The following table shows a reflexive verb given in all of its present tense conjugations.

reflexive pronoun + bañarse = to bathe (oneself)	
me baño	nos bañamos
te bañas	os bañáis
se baña	se bañan
Yo me **baño.** = I *bathe* myself.	

Many of these reflexive verbs involve the mention of a body part, and because it's already clear to whom the body part belongs (because of the reflexive verb), you don't use a possessive pronoun. Instead of saying, "I brush my hair," for example, you'd say, "I brush the hair," because the reflexive pronoun already signals that it's your hair.

Two verbs that are used reflexively but vary slightly from the general definition of a reflexive verb are **irse,** which when used reflexively, means to *go away,* and the verb **comerse,** which doesn't mean *to eat oneself* but rather *to gobble up.*

Table 3-5 gives a list of some commonly used reflexive verbs:

Table 3-5	Common Reflexive Verbs
Spanish Verb (Used with a Reflexive Pronoun)	*English Translation*
afeitarse	to shave oneself
bañarse	to bathe oneself
casarse (con alguien)	to get married; to marry (someone)
cepillarse — el pelo — los dientes	to brush oneself — hair — teeth
ducharse	to take a shower
enfermarse	to get sick
enojarse	to get angry; mad
irse	to go away
lavarse	to wash oneself
levantarse	to stand up; get up
llamarse	to call oneself
mirarse	to look at oneself
peinarse	to comb one's hair
ponerse	to become
ponerse la ropa	to put on (clothing)
preocuparse por	to worry (about)

Spanish Verb (Used with a Reflexive Pronoun)	English Translation
quitarse	to take off, remove (clothing)
secarse	to dry oneself
verse	to see oneself

Translate the following statements into Spanish, as I show you below. Each one includes a reflexive verb. Remember to place the reflexive pronoun in front of the conjugated verb.

He looks at himself in the mirror frequently. = *Él se mira en el espejo frecuentamente.*

81. I take a bath every day.

_____

82. He dries himself after he showers (himself).

_____

83. Raúl shaves in the morning.

_____

84. She brushes her hair a lot.

_____

85. They take a bath at night.

_____

86. We brush our teeth every day.

_____

87. I get sick a lot when I travel.

_____

88. He gets up at 7 a.m. every day.

_____

89. The teacher gets angry with the students sometimes.

_____

90. The students take showers after P.E. class.

_____

Having It All with Tener

The verb **tener** is a simple irregular verb that's basically used to express possession, such as "I have a new car," or "Pedro has a dog named Sam." But it's deceptively basic and extremely versatile. You combine **tener** with other verbs to express a desire or obligation to take action. You can also use it to express age — how young or how old you are. In short, you can get a lot of mileage out of this unassuming verb.

Use the following chart to drill yourself on the present tense forms of **tener.**

tener = to have	
tengo	**tenemos**
tienes	**tenéis**
tiene	**tienen**
Uds. **tienen.** = You (plural, formal) *have.*	

Expressing desire or obligation with tener

You can use **tener** to create additional verb structures that express desire or obligation. The following instructions explain how to create each verb structure:

- To express desire, or say that someone *feels like* doing something, take the form of **tener** that agrees with the subject of your sentence and then add **ganas de** + infinitive.

- To express obligation, or say that someone *has to* perform an action, take the form of **tener** that agrees with the subject of your sentence and then add **que** + infinitive.

Here are a few examples to show you how these two structures work.

Yo tengo ganas de ir de compras. = I feel like going shopping.

Ella tiene ganas de cantar. = She feels like singing.

Ellos tienen que estudiar. = They have to study.

Él tiene que trabajar hoy. = He has to work today.

Telling your age with tener

When someone asks you how old you are, **tener** can help you answer the question. Take the correct conjugated form for whomever you are describing and then give the correct number of years that that person *has,* or as you'd say in English, "is."

The following examples should help you phrase your answer to questions about age:

Yo tengo veinte años. = I am 20. (literally translates as "I have 20 years")

Ella tiene treinta y cinco años. = She is 35.

In Spanish, it's not about how old you *are* but how many years you *have.*

Translate the following sentences into Spanish. They all contain the verb **tener** (to have) either by itself or in one of the structures that I describe in the previous sections.

91. We have a new car.

_____

92. They have to study this afternoon.

_____

93. I have three cats and two dogs.

_____

94. Juan feels like playing soccer today.

_____

95. The students don't feel like studying.

_____

96. She has to wash the dishes every day.

_____

97. We feel like walking in the park.

_____

98. Rafael is 43 years old.

_____

99. My grandfather has four brothers and two sisters.

_____

100. My mother has to clean the house today.

_____

Answer Key

Write the following **tú** form commands in Spanish.

1. Open the window.

Abre la ventana.

2. Sing.

Canta.

3. Don't watch TV.

No mires la televisión.

4. Leave.

Sal.

5. Don't be foolish!

¡No seas tonto!

6. Dance.

Baila.

7. Listen to the teacher.

Escucha a la profesora.

8. Deal the cards.

Reparte los naipes.

9. Don't bore the students.

No aburras a los estudiantes.

10. Don't leave late.

No salgas tarde.

11. Wash the dishes.

Lava los platos.

12. Clean the house.

Limpia la casa.

13. Run.

Corre.

14. Walk.

    Camina.

15. Talk louder.

    Habla más alto.

16. Study for the exam.

    Estudia para el examen.

17. Describe your house.

    Describe su casa.

18. Do not attend the concert.

    No asistas el concierto.

19. Do not surprise the children.

    No sorprendas a los niños.

20. Read the newspaper every day.

    Lee el periódico todos los días.

21. Put the book on the table.

    Pon el libro en la mesa.

22. Celebrate!

    ¡Celebra!

23. Don't come early.

    No vengas temprano.

24. Don't do the homework today.

    No hagas la tarea hoy.

25. Don't break the dishes!

    ¡No rompas los platos!

    Write the following **Ud.** commands in Spanish.

26. Play the piano.

    Toque el piano.

27. Don't sing this song.

No cante esta canción.

28. Walk to the store.

Camine a la tienda.

29. Run fast.

Corra rápido.

30. Don't study all the time.

No estudie todo el tiempo.

31. Don't eat dinner now.

No cene ahora.

32. Help the students.

Ayude a los estudiantes.

33. Don't eat before dinner.

No coma antes de la cena.

34. Prepare the lesson.

Prepare la lección.

35. Wash the dishes.

Lave los platos.

Write the following **Uds.** commands in Spanish.

36. Go to bed.

Vayan a la cama.

37. Be good.

Sean buenos.

38. Clean your rooms.

Limpien sus cuartos.

39. Help the teacher.

Ayuden a la profesora.

40. Don't run in the school.

    No corran en la escuela.

41. Eat the dinner.

    Coman la cena.

42. Cut the paper.

    Corten el papel.

43. Read the story.

    Lean el cuento.

44. Sing louder.

    Canten más alto.

45. Talk to the manager.

    Hablen al gerente.

    Write the following **vosotros** form commands in Spanish.

46. Chat with your friends.

    Charlad con vuestros amigos.

47. Don't talk on the phone so much.

    No habléis por teléfono tanto.

48. Go to the store.

    Id a la tienda.

49. Don't believe everything that they say.

    No creáis todo lo que dicen.

50. Eat all of your food.

    Comed toda la comida.

51. Tell the truth.

    Decid la verdad.

52. Dance at the party.

    Bailad en la fiesta.

53. Sell all of the old books.

Vended todos los libros viejos.

54. Don't talk to the other students during the test.

No habléis a los otros estudiantes durante el examen.

55. Win the game.

Ganad el partido.

Put the following *Let's* form commands in Spanish.

56. Let's write.

Escribamos.

57. Let's go to the movie.

Vamos a la película.

58. Let's listen to the radio.

Escuchemos la radio.

59. Let's walk faster.

Caminemos más rápido.

60. Let's read to the students.

Leamos a los estudiantes.

61. Let's help our parents.

Ayudemos a nuestros padres.

62. Let's dance.

Bailemos.

63. Let's buy new books.

Compremos libros nuevos.

64. Let's clean the house later.

Limpiemos la casa más tarde.

65. Let's talk on the phone tomorrow.

Hablemos por teléfono mañana.

66. Let's not break the dishes.

No rompamos los platos.

67. Let's walk to the store.

    Caminemos a la tienda.

68. Let's not draw in the dictionary.

    No dibujemos en el diccionario.

69. Let's not clean the house today.

    No limpiemos la casa hoy.

70. Let's celebrate this weekend.

    Celebremos este fin de semana.

    Write the following present progressive sentences in Spanish.

71. She is buying a new car.

    Ella está comprando un carro nuevo.

72. They are singing at the concert.

    Ellos están cantando en el concierto.

73. We are eating in a French restaurant.

    Nosotros estamos comiendo en un restaurante francés.

74. Juan is listening to his radio.

    Juan está escuchando su radio.

75. I am walking my dog in the park.

    Yo estoy caminando a mi perro en el parque.

76. The mechanic is repairing the car.

    El mecánico está reparando el carro.

77. They are reading the newspaper.

    Ellos están leyendo el periódico.

78. We are discussing the new verbs.

    Nosotros estamos discutiendo los verbos nuevos.

79. Susana is shopping at the new mall.

    Susana está yendo de compras en el centro comercial nuevo.

80. My mother is preparing dinner.

    Mi madre está preparando la cena.

Translate the following statements into Spanish. All include reflexive verbs.

81. I take a bath every day.

    Yo me baño todos los días.

82. He dries himself after he showers (himself).

    Él se seca después de que se ducha.

83. Raúl shaves in the morning.

    Raúl se afeita por la mañana.

84. She brushes her hair a lot.

    Ella se cepilla el pelo mucho.

85. They take a bath at night.

    Ellos se bañan por la noche.

86. We brush our teeth every day.

    Nosotros nos cepillamos los dientes todos los días.

87. I get sick a lot when I travel.

    Yo me enfermo mucho cuando yo viajo.

88. He gets up at 7 a.m. every day.

    Él se levanta a las siete todos los días.

89. The teacher gets angry with the students sometimes.

    La profesora se enoja con los estudiantes a veces.

90. The students take showers after P.E. class.

    Los estudiantes se duchan después de la clase de educación física.

Translate the following sentences into Spanish. They all contain the verb **tener** (to have).

91. We have a new car.

    Nosotros tenemos un carro nuevo.

92. They have to study this afternoon.

    Ellos tienen que estudiar esta tarde.

93. I have three cats and two dogs.

    Yo tengo tres gatos y dos perros.

94. Juan feels like playing soccer today.

Juan tiene ganas de jugar a fútbol hoy.

95. The students don't feel like studying.

Los estudiantes no tienen ganas de estudiar.

96. She has to wash the dishes every day.

Ella tiene que lavar los platos todos los días.

97. We feel like walking in the park.

Nosotros tenemos ganas de caminar en el parque.

98. Rafael is 43 years old.

Rafael tiene cuarenta y tres años.

99. My grandfather has four brothers and two sisters.

Mi abuelo tiene cuatro hermanos y dos hermanas.

100. My mother has to clean the house today.

Mi madre tiene que limpiar la casa hoy.

Chapter 4

Popping the Questions

*W*hen your inquiring mind wants to know something, it asks questions. You may ask *yes/no* questions. Did you go to the concert last night? Did you drive? Did you have a good time? Did you commit a felony? Or you may ask more specific, *interrogative* questions, such as: What time did the concert start? Where was it? Who was the main performer? Why did the police have to drive you home? You need to know how to phrase those questions and how to answer them.

In this chapter, I tell you how to structure yes/no and interrogative questions; restructure a statement to form a question; use common interrogative words, such as *who, what, when, where,* and *why;* and answer yes/no and interrogative questions. If you still have questions after you complete this chapter, at least you'll know how to ask them.

Asking a Yes/No Question (for Lawyers Only)

Lawyers love yes/no questions because they leave no wiggle room. A witness is on the stand, and the lawyer asks a question to which only two answers are acceptable — yes or no. But yes/no questions also are suitable for other situations. If you want to know whether someone knows something, you can ask a yes/no question before getting into the particulars. Yes/no questions enable you to cut to the chase.

In English, when you ask a yes/no question in the present tense, you often begin with either *do* or *does.* For example: Do you like ice cream? Does she wear makeup? When forming a yes/no question in Spanish, however, you don't need to add anything. You simply take a simple statement and invert (switch the places of) the subject and the verb. Of course, you have to add the question marks — both of them — one at the beginning and one at the end. You can see what I mean in the following examples:

Él tiene un carro nuevo. = ¿Tiene él un carro nuevo?

Ellos bailan muy bien. = ¿Bailan ellos muy bien?

Make the following statements into questions by inverting the subject and the verb, as I show you in the following example:

Él trabaja aquí. = *¿Trabaja él aquí?*

REMEMBER

Spanish uses question marks at the beginning (upside down) and the end of questions.

1. El profesor tiene diez libros.

   _____

2. Su mamá prepara la cena a las seis.

   _____

3. Ellos hablan por teléfono todos los días.

   _____

4. Los estudiantes estudian mucho durante los fines de semana.

   _____

5. Él canta muy bien.

   _____

6. María y Pilar bailan en la fiesta.

   _____

7. Ella decide ir a la biblioteca con sus amigos.

   _____

8. Francisco lava los platos a veces.

   _____

9. Ellos leen el periódico en la biblioteca.

   _____

10. Rafael camina a su perro en el parque.

    _____

Answering a Yes/No Question with a Yes/No Answer

To say *yes* in Spanish, say, **"Sí."** No is **"No."** For the sake of clarity and emphasis, however, you may want to include a portion of the question in your answer. Doing so has the added benefit of proving that you were, in fact, listening.

To answer positively, open your statement with **sí** and then follow up with the statement you're supporting. To answer negatively, start with saying, **"No, (subject) no . . ."** followed by the statement that you're negating. The subject is in parentheses because you don't always have to include it in Spanish if the information already is clear.

Here's an example of a question answered positively and negatively:

Question	**¿Baila Raúl mucho?** = Does Raúl dance a lot?
Positive response	**Sí, Raúl baila mucho.** = Yes, Raúl dances a lot.
Negative response	**No, Raúl no baila mucho.** = No, Raúl doesn't dance a lot.

Supply answers to the questions in the affirmative or negative as specified below. Here's an example to get you started:

¿Trabaja él aquí? = No, *he does not work here.*

11. ¿Tiene el profesor diez libros?

Sí, _____

12. ¿Prepara su mamá la cena a las seis?

Sí,_____

13. ¿Hablan ellos por teléfono todos los días?

No, _____

14. ¿Estudian los estudiantes mucho durante los fines de semana?

Sí, _____

15. ¿Canta él muy bien?

No, _____

16. ¿Bailan María y Pilar en la fiesta?

No, _____

17. ¿Decide ella ir a la biblioteca con sus amigos?

No, _____

18. ¿Lava Francisco los platos a veces?

Sí, _____

19. ¿Leen ellos el periódico en la biblioteca?

Sí,_____

20. ¿Camina Rafael a su perro en el parque?

No, _____

Posing Interrogative Questions Inquiring Minds Want to Know

An experienced news reporter knows the importance of the five major interrogatives: *Who? What? When? Where?* and *Why?* If the reporter can obtain solid answers to those five questions, he or she has everything necessary to put together a Pulitzer Prize winning piece. Those five interrogative words are a good start in Spanish, too, but you also need to familiarize yourself with some additional interrogative words. Table 4-1 reveals the most important interrogative words in English and Spanish.

Table 4-1	Interrogative Words
Spanish Interrogative Words	*Translation*
¿Quién(es) . . . ?	Who . . . ?
¿Qué . . . ?	What . . . ?
¿Dónde . . . ?	Where . . . ?
¿Adónde . . . ?	Where (to) . . . ?
¿De dónde . . . ?	Where (from) . . . ?
¿Cuándo . . . ?	When . . . ?
¿Cómo . . . ?	How . . . ?
¿Porqué . . . ?	Why . . . ?
¿Cuánto/a . . . ?	How much . . . ?
¿Cuántos/as . . . ?	How many . . . ?

To form a question with the interrogative words, you follow the same inversion rule that you use when forming a yes/no question, but then you tack on the interrogative word at the beginning, and of course, add the question marks. If you want to know when Susana dances well, for example, here's how you would phrase your question:

Susana baila muy bien. = Susana dances really well.

¿Cuándo baila Susana muy bien? = When does Susana dance really well?

To inquire who dances really well, simply omit Susana's name and rephrase your question as follows:

¿Quién baila muy bien? = Who dances really well?

To find out how Susana dances, use the interrogative word **cómo** to structure your interrogative question in the following way:

¿Cómo baila Susana? = How does Susana dance?

In an interrogative question, the interrogative word is first, followed by the verb and then any other information that is pertinent to convey the information about which you want to inquire.

Ask these interrogative style questions in Spanish. I've used the information from the first ten practice sentences in this section to form these questions, so you may find it useful to refer to them as you write your questions.

Here's a sample translation:

Where does he work? = *¿Dónde trabaja él?*

21. How many books does the professor have?

_____

22. Who prepares dinner at 6 p.m.?

_____

23. When do they talk on the phone?

_____

24. When do the students study a lot?

_____

25. How does he sing?

_____

26. Where do Pilar and María dance?

_____

27. Where (to) does she decide to go with her friends?

_____

28. What does Francisco wash sometimes?

_____

29. Who (plural) reads the newspaper in the library?

_____

30. Where does Rafael walk his dog?

_____

Coming up with Some Answers

The easiest way to answer an interrogative question is to recycle the material — rephrase the question as a statement and tack on the specific information your interrogator requested. In the previous section, interrogative questions were formed out of statements by omitting the information that you were seeking and adding an interrogative word at the front of the question. To answer these same questions, you simply reverse the process by:

1. **Omitting the interrogative word.**

2. **Inverting the question into a statement.**

3. **Adding the details.**

So if you want to know when Juan studies, and the answer is every day, the question and answer will look like this:

¿Cuándo estudia Juan? = Juan estudia todos los días.

Now say, for example, you want to know who studies every day. You omit Juan's name and add *who* instead of *when* as your interrogative. The Q&A then looks like this:

¿Quién estudia todos los días? = Juan estudia todos los días.

The plural *who* (**¿Quiénes . . . ?**) is used when the suspected answer is more than one person. When using the plural *who*, the Q&A takes on the following appearance:

¿Quiénes estudian todos los días? = Juan y Antonio estudian todos los días.

Answer the following interrogative questions in Spanish by using the information from the statements in the first activity in this chapter under "Asking a Yes/No Question (for Lawyers Only)."

Here's one to get you started:

¿Dónde trabaja él? = *Él trabaja aquí.*

31. ¿Cuántos libros tiene el profesor?

_____

32. ¿Quién prepara la cena a las seis?

_____

33. ¿Cuándo hablan por teléfono?

_____

34. ¿Cuándo estudian mucho los estudiantes?

_____

35. ¿Cómo canta él?

   _____

36. ¿Dónde bailan Pilar y María?

   _____

37. ¿Adónde decide ella ir con sus amigos?

   _____

38. ¿Qué lava Francisco a veces?

   _____

39. ¿Quiénes leen el periódico en la biblioteca?

   _____

40. ¿Dónde camina Rafael a su perro?

   _____

Answer Key

Make the following statements into questions by inverting the subject and the verb.

Spanish uses question marks at the beginning and at the end of questions.

1. El profesor tiene diez libros.

   ¿Tiene el profesor diez libros?

2. Su mamá prepara la cena a las seis.

   ¿Prepara su mamá la cena a las seis?

3. Ellos hablan por teléfono todos los días.

   ¿Hablan ellos por teléfono todos los días?

4. Los estudiantes estudian mucho durante los fines de semana.

   ¿Estudian los estudiantes mucho durante los fines de semana?

5. Él canta muy bien.

   ¿Canta él muy bien?

6. María y Pilar bailan en la fiesta.

   ¿Bailan María y Pilar en la fiesta?

7. Ella decide ir a la biblioteca con sus amigos.

   ¿Decide ella ir a la biblioteca con sus amigos?

8. Francisco lava los platos a veces.

   ¿Lava Francisco los platos a veces?

9. Ellos leen el periódico en la biblioteca.

   ¿Leen ellos el periódico en la biblioteca?

10. Rafael camina a su perro en el parque.

    ¿Camina Rafael a su perro en el parque?

Supply answers to the questions in the affirmative or negative as specified.

11. ¿Tiene el profesor diez libros?

    Sí, *el profesor tiene diez libros.*

12. ¿Prepara su mamá la cena a las seis?

    Sí, *su mamá prepara la cena a las seis.*

13. ¿Hablan ellos por teléfono todos los días?

    No, *ellos no hablan por teléfono todos los días.*

14. ¿Estudian los estudiantes mucho durante los fines de semana?

Sí, *los estudiantes estudian mucho durante los fines de semana.*

15. ¿Canta él muy bien?

No, *él no canta muy bien.*

16. ¿Bailan María y Pilar en la fiesta?

No, *María y Pilar no bailan en la fiesta.*

17. ¿Decide ella ir a la biblioteca con sus amigos?

No, *ella no decide ir a la biblioteca con sus amigos.*

18. ¿Lava Francisco los platos a veces?

Sí, *Francisco lava los platos a veces.*

19. ¿Leen ellos el periódico en la biblioteca?

Sí, *ellos leen el periódico en la biblioteca.*

20. ¿Camina Rafael a su perro en el parque?

No, *Rafael no camina a su perro en el parque.*

Ask these interrogative style questions in Spanish. I've used the information from the first ten practice sentences in this section to form these questions, so you may find it useful to refer to them as you write your questions.

21. How many books does the professor have?

¿Cuántos libros tiene el profesor?

22. Who prepares dinner at six?

¿Quién prepara la cena a las seis?

23. When do they talk on the phone?

¿Cuándo hablan ellos por teléfono?

24. When do the students study a lot?

¿Cuándo estudian los estudiantes mucho?

25. How does he sing?

¿Cómo canta él?

26. Where do Pilar and María dance?

¿Dónde bailan Pilar y María?

27. Where (to) does she decide to go with her friends?

¿Adónde decide ella ir con sus amigos?

28. What does Francisco wash sometimes?

¿Qué lava Francisco a veces?

29. Who (plural) reads the newspaper in the library?

¿Quiénes leen el periódico en la biblioteca?

30. Where does Rafael walk his dog?

¿Dónde camina Rafael a su perro?

Answer the following interrogative questions using the information from the statements in the first activity in this chapter under "Asking a Yes/No Question (for Lawyers Only)."

31. ¿Cuántos libros tiene el profesor?

El profesor tiene diez libros.

32. ¿Quién prepara la cena a las seis?

Su mamá prepara la cena a las seis.

33. ¿Cuándo hablan por teléfono?

Ellos hablan por teléfono todos los días.

34. ¿Cuándo estudian mucho los estudiantes?

Los estudiantes estudian mucho durante los fines de semana.

35. ¿Cómo canta él?

Él canta muy bien.

36. ¿Dónde bailan Pilar y María?

María y Pilar bailan en la fiesta.

37. ¿Adónde decide ella ir con sus amigos?

Ella decide ir a la biblioteca con sus amigos.

38. ¿Qué lava Francisco a veces?

Francisco lava los platos a veces.

39. ¿Quiénes leen el periódico en la biblioteca?

Ellos leen el periódico en la biblioteca.

40. ¿Dónde camina Rafael a su perro?

Rafael camina a su perro en el parque.

Chapter 5

Coming and Going with *Venir* and *Ir*

In This Chapter

▶ Going once, going twice, with the verb **ir**

▶ Introducing the verb **venir**

▶ Contracting the prepositions **a** and **de**

Do you ever get that feeling that you don't know whether you're coming or going? Well, in this chapter, you get to do both with the Spanish verbs **venir** (to come) and **ir** (to go). Although these verbs are two of the tiniest in the Spanish language, they're also two of the most commonly used and irregular verbs, and they demand special attention in this book.

In this chapter, not only do you find out how to express your goings and comings in Spanish, but you also discover how to do it in all of the present-tense forms. And because you're always coming *from* somewhere or going *to* someplace, you also find out how to use these prepositions to describe where it is you're coming from or going to.

Going the Distance with *Ir*

The verb **ir** is definitely the smallest **-ir** type verb, and that's really all it is — an *i* and an *r*. Actually, it looks like a verb without a verb stem, an end with no beginning. It's also one of the most irregular verbs in the Spanish language. As you can see from its conjugation chart, the verb **ir** gives the term *irregular* a whole new meaning. Who would ever think that *going* could be so complicated?

ir = to go	
voy	**vamos**
vas	**vais**
va	**van**
Nosotros **vamos.** = We *go*.	

Spend some time drilling the verb forms into your brain cells, and then when you think you have them down, proceed to the following exercise to test your skills.

Provide the correct form of the verb **ir** for the following subjects, as I show you here:

Mi papá = *va*

1. Tomás = _____

2. nosotros = _____

3. yo = _____

4. mis amigos = _____

5. los estudiantes = _____

6. Pilar = _____

7. ellas = _____

8. tú = _____

9. vosotros = _____

10. Uds. = _____

Coming Around with Venir

People come and people go.

The verb **venir** covers the coming end of the equation. Although the verb **venir** isn't quite as irregular as **ir**, it's still fairly irregular, as the following conjugation chart shows.

venir = to come	
vengo	venimos
vienes	venís
viene	vienen
Uds. **vienen.** = You (plural, formal) *come.*	

Spend some time drilling the **venir** verb forms, and then when you think you have them down, proceed to the following exercise to test your skills.

Provide the correct form of the verb **venir** to say that the following people are coming. Here's an example to get you started:

Los estudiantes = *vienen*

11. yo = _____

12. mis amigos = _____

13. ellos = _____

14. Uds. = _____

15. Alicia = _____

16. mi hermana = _____

17. tú = _____

18. vosotras = _____

19. Raúl y yo = _____

20. el profesor = _____

Contracting a and de — Only When You Must

Whenever you talk about coming and going you need to use the prepositions **a** (*to* in English) and **de** (*from* in English), because you will always be going to or coming from some-place. When using these prepositions in Spanish, you first need to become acquainted with one crucial rule: Whenever **a** or **de** precedes the masculine singular article **el,** you must con-tract the preposition. When **a** precedes **el,** the two contract to form **al.** When **de** precedes **el,** the two contract to form **del.** The following examples help drive the point home:

> **Yo voy (a + el parque) al parque.** = I am going to the park.
>
> **Nosotros vamos (a + el restaurante)** = We are going to the Mexican restaurant.
> **al restaurante mexicano.**
>
> **Ellos vienen (de + el cine) del cine.** = They are coming from the cinema.
>
> **Él viene (de + el teatro) del teatro.** = He is coming from the theater.

These contractions, **al** and **del,** occur only with the masculine singular article **el.**

Translate the following sentences into Spanish, using the verbs **ir** and **venir** and the prepo-sitions **a** and **de,** as I show you here:

We are going to a restaurant tonight.

Nosotros vamos a un restaurante esta noche.

21. Rodolfo and Marisol are coming from the beach.

_____

22. We go to the theater sometimes.

_____

23. They go to the beach a lot.

_____

24. My mother is going to the supermarket now.

_____

25. Her parents are coming from the gym.

_____

26. You (familiar) are coming from the university.

   _____

27. She goes to church every Sunday.

   _____

28. I am coming from the auditorium.

   _____

29. Pedro is going to the airport now.

   _____

30. You (plural) are going to the cinema this weekend. Right?

   _____

Answer Key

Provide the correct form of the verb **ir** for the following subjects.

1. Tomás = *va*

2. nosotros = *vamos*

3. yo = *voy*

4. mis amigos = *van*

5. los estudiantes = *van*

6. Pilar = *va*

7. ellas = *van*

8. tú = *van*

9. vosotros = *vais*

10. Uds. = *van*

Provide the correct form of the verb **venir** to say that the following people are coming.

11. yo = *vengo*

12. mis amigos = *vienen*

13. ellos = *vienen*

14. Uds. = *vienen*

15. Alicia = *viene*

16. mi hermana = *viene*

17. tú = *vienes*

18. vosotras = *venís*

19. Raúl y yo = *venimos*

20. el profesor = *viene*

Translate the following sentences into Spanish, using the verbs **ir** and **venir** and the prepositions **a** and **de.**

21. Rodolfo and Marisol are coming from the beach.

    Rodolfo y Marisol vienen de la playa.

22. We go to the theater sometimes.

    Nosotros vamos al teatro a veces.

23. They go to the beach a lot.

    Ellos van a la playa mucho.

24. My mother is going to the supermarket now.

    Mi madre va al supermercado ahora.

25. Her parents are coming from the gym.

    Sus padres vienen del gimnasio.

26. You (familiar) are coming from the university.

    Tú vienes de la universidad.

27. She goes to church every Sunday.

    Ella va a la iglesia todos los domingos.

28. I am coming from the auditorium.

    Yo vengo del auditorio.

29. Pedro is going to the airport now.

    Pedro va al aeropuerto ahora.

30. You (plural) are going to the cinema this weekend. Right?

    Uds. van al cine este fin de semana. ¿Verdad?

Part II
Exploring Some Exceptional Exceptions

The 5th Wave — By Rich Tennant

"Stop, stop, stop! I told you not to call a square dance in Spanish until you had the verbs down!"

In this part . . .

Just when you thought you had this verb thing under control, the language throws its exceptions at you. In this case, I'm talking about the verbs that refuse to conform to the standard rules and regulations that govern conjugations. The Spanish language features a couple notable exceptions, including the verb **gustar** (for expressing your likes and dislikes), **ser** (for describing the essence of a person, place, or thing), and **estar** (for describing the temporary condition or location of a person, place, or thing). Spanish also has some stem-changing and spelling-changing verbs to further confuse you.

In this part, you find out how to describe who you are, what you do, where you're from, and what you like and dislike. I even show you how to hold your own in a conversation about the weather.

Chapter 6

Declaring Your Likes and Dislikes with *Gustar*

When it comes to liking and disliking something, English and Spanish have a slightly different way of expressing what's going on. In English, the subject of the sentence is in charge of liking or disliking something. You may say, "I like vanilla ice cream," or, "I don't like red sports cars." In Spanish, the object of your desire, or lack of desire, is more responsible for pleasing you. Instead of saying, "I like vanilla ice cream," you say, "Vanilla ice cream is pleasing to me" — **"Me gusta el helado de vainilla."**

In Spanish, rather than looking for the subject at the beginning of the sentence to determine the verb form, you look to the object at the end of the sentence. The object is in control of the action. This chapter introduces you to an entire group of verbs with a variety of meanings that share this reverse formation process and use indirect-object pronouns to clarify the *who* in the sentence.

Taking on Indirect-Object Pronouns

Before I get started explaining the finer points of a complicated Spanish verb **gustar,** I need to let you in on the secret of indirect-object pronouns, because you need them when you work with **gustar** and other verbs like it.

An *indirect object* is anything or anyone that the action of a sentence affects in an indirect way. If you kick your friend Sally the ball, for example, *the ball* is the *direct object* because it's getting kicked, and *Sally* is the indirect object. When you use the indirect object, you're saying you're kicking the ball "to Sally."

A *pronoun* is a word that stands in for a specific name or noun. Think of it as the generic brand. So if instead of saying you "kicked your friend Sally the ball," you said you "kicked her the ball," you'd be using an indirect object pronoun — *her*. The indirect-object pronoun usually implies the word *to* or *for*. Spanish uses the indirect-object pronouns in the table that follows.

Indirect Object Pronouns	
me = to me	**nos** = to us
te = to you (familiar)	**os** = to you (plural, familiar)
le = to him, her, you (formal)	**les** = to them, you (plural, formal)

When you use one of these indirect-object pronouns in a Spanish sentence, be sure to place it *in front of* the conjugated verb.

Take Your Pick: Gusta or Gustan?

In Spanish, expressions of like and dislike are completely flip-flopped when compared to English. You use the verb **gustar** for the verb *to like* in English, but **gustar** really means *to be pleasing to*. When you form a sentence, then, whatever is doing the pleasing becomes the subject and determines the form of the verb **gustar.** Use the following rules as your guide:

✔ If you like a single thing, use the third-person singular form, **gusta.**

✔ If you like two or more things, use the third-person plural form, **gustan.**

✔ If you like to do activities and you're using verbs to describe those activities, use the third-person singular form. Stick with the third-person singular, even if you like multiple activities.

✔ Use indirect-object pronouns to clarify to whom the thing (subject) is pleasing. If you need further clarification, place a clause with **a** and the name of the person at the beginning of your sentence.

To see how this plays out in real life, check out the following example:

> *Sentence:* **A Juan le gusta el restaurante Mexicano.**
>
> *Literal translation:* To Juan, to him, is pleasing the Mexican restaurant.
>
> *Real-life translation:* Juan likes the Mexican restaurant.

A Juan is used here to clarify who is indicated by the pronoun **le.** Sometimes you need prepositional phrases only for emphasis, rather than clarity. For example, if I was telling you about something that I liked, you'd know that the Spanish indirect-object pronoun **me** was me, but I can emphasize that I *really* liked it by adding, **a mí** at the front of my sentence.

Here's a sentence with a plural subject. Remember, the subject is at the end of the sentence.

> *Sentence:* **A ellos les gustan las películas.**
>
> *Literal translation:* To them are pleasing movies.
>
> *Real-life translation:* They like movies.

You simply put a **no** in front of the indirect-object pronoun — after the clarifying clause — to make a negative statement with the verb **gustar** and other similar verbs. So for example:

> **A él no le gusta pescar.** = He doesn't like to fish.

You can add **mucho** after the verb to say that you *really* like something. For example:

> **A ella le gusta mucho bailar.** = She really likes dancing.

Translate the following sentences into Spanish. Remember to use clarifying clauses with the preposition **a** at the beginning of your sentences. Use **gusta** with singular subjects and verbs and **gustan** with plural subjects, as I show you here:

The children like candy. = *A los niños les gustan los dulces.*

1. She likes dogs.

_____

2. They like to dance.

_____

3. He doesn't like to wash the dishes.

_____

4. We like to sing.

_____

5. I really like ice cream.

_____

Brushing up on Other Verbs Like Gustar

You have to admit that **gustar** is out of the norm as far as Spanish verbs go, but it isn't a one-of-a-kind wonder. The verb **gustar** is a member of an exclusive organization of verbs that include verbs that mean *repugnant to, fascinating to,* and *interesting to.*

Conjugating these verbs is a snap. You can forget, for a moment anyway, all you learned about first- and second-person singular and plural. All these verbs conjugate just like **gustar,** using indirect-object pronouns and the third-person singular and plural forms. Table 6-1 shows the most commonly used **gustar** look-alikes along with their meanings.

Table 6-1	Verbs Conjugated in the Third Person with Indirect Objects
Spanish Verb	*Translation*
disgustar	to be repugnant to
encantar	to be enchanting to
faltar	to be lacking to
fascinar	to be fascinating to
importar	to be important to
interesar	to be interesting to
molestar	to bother
parecer	to seem; to appear to

The **-ar** verbs above use either the endings **-a** or **-an.** The verb **parecer,** which is the only **-er** verb, uses the endings **-e** or **-en.**

Using all of the verbs from Table 6-1 and the verb **gustar,** translate the following sentences into Spanish. Here's an example to get you started:

I love pizza. = *A mí me encanta el pizza.*

6. Chess is interesting to Juana.

    _____

7. They are fascinated by birds.

    _____

8. The students need books. (Books are lacking to the students.)

    _____

9. The Italian restaurant seems very good to us.

    _____

10. It is very important to me to work a lot.

    _____

11. The boys like playing soccer. (Playing soccer is pleasing to the boys.)

    _____

12. He is lacking enough money to go (in order to go) to Europe.

    _____

13. My father is enchanted by classical music.

    _____

14. Lola is bothered by her younger brothers every day.

    _____

15. You (plural, formal) need pencils. Right?

    _____

Answer the following statements either *C* for *cierto* (true) or *F* for *falso* (false), based on your beliefs, likes, and dislikes. Here's an example:

C A mí me gustan los conciertos de rock. *(I like rock concerts.)*

16. _____ A mí me encanta la música clásica.

17. _____ A mí me gusta ir a la playa en el verano.

18. _____ A mí me fascina el álgebra.

19. _____ A mí me molestan los niños difíciles.

20. _____ A mí me interesa la política.

21. _____ A mí me importa mucho votar.

22. _____ A mí me parece fácil la química.

23. _____ A mí me fascina viajar a lugares diferentes.

24. _____ A mí me disgustan las películas de horror.

25. _____ A mí me interesan mucho los museos de arte.

Answer Key

Translate the following sentences into Spanish. Remember to use clarifying clauses with the preposition **a** at the beginning of your sentences. Use **gusta** with singular subjects and verbs and **gustan** with plural subjects.

1. She likes dogs.

   A ella le gustan los perros.

2. They like to dance.

   A ellos les gusta bailar.

3. He doesn't like to wash the dishes.

   A él no le gusta lavar los platos.

4. We like to sing.

   A nosotros nos gusta cantar.

5. I really like ice cream.

   A mí me gusta mucho el helado.

Using all of the verbs above and the verb **gustar,** translate the following sentences into Spanish.

6. Chess is interesting to Juana.

   A Juana le interesa el ajedrez.

7. They are fascinated by birds.

   A ellos les fascinan los pájaros.

8. The students need books. (Books are lacking to the students.)

   A los estudiantes les faltan libros.

9. The Italian restaurant seems very good to us.

   A nosotros nos parece muy bueno el restaurante italiano.

10. It is very important to me to work a lot.

    A mí me importa trabajar mucho.

11. The boys like playing soccer. (Playing soccer is pleasing to the boys.)

    A los muchachos les gusta jugar al fútbol.

12. He is lacking enough money to go (in order to go) to Europe.

A él le falta bastante dinero para ir a Europa.

13. My father is enchanted by classical music.

A mi padre le encanta la música clásica.

14. Lola is bothered by her younger brothers every day.

A Lola le molestan sus hermanos menores todos los días.

15. You (plural, formal) need pencils. Right?

A Uds. les faltan lápices. ¿Verdad?

Answer the following statements either *C* for *cierto* (true) or *F* for *falso* (false), based on your beliefs, likes, and dislikes. Because these answers are a matter of opinion, I simply provide the translations for you.

16. *C/F* A mí me encanta la música clásica. *(I love classical music.)*

17. *C/F* A mí me gusta ir a la playa en el verano. *(I like going to the beach in the summer.)*

18. *C/F* A mí me fascina el álgebra. *(Algebra fascinates me.)*

19. *C/F* A mí me molestan los niños difíciles. *(Difficult children bother me.)*

20. *C/F* A mí me interesa la política. *(Politics interests me.)*

21. *C/F* A mí me importa mucho votar. *(Voting is very [really] important to me.)*

22. *C/F* A mí me parece fácil la química. *(Chemistry seems easy to me.)*

23. *C/F* A mí me fascina viajar a lugares diferentes. *(Traveling to different places fascinates me.)*

24. *C/F* A mí me disgustan las películas de horror. *(I hate horror movies.)*

25. *C/F* A mí me interesan mucho los museos de arte. *(Art museums really interest me.)*

Chapter 7

Being All That You Can Be with *Ser* and *Estar*

In This Chapter

▶ Describing the unchanging nature of a person, place, or thing with **ser**

▶ Expressing the ever-changing being of a person, place, or thing with **estar**

▶ Discerning the subtle nuances of **ser** and **estar**

The concept of being is quite simple — unless, of course, you happen to be an armchair philosopher. Sometimes philosophers become so obsessed with the concept of being that they begin to question their own being. They have to come up with quotes (like Descartes's "I think, therefore I am") just to be able to acknowledge their own existence.

In this chapter, I won't get quite that obsessed with the concept of being, but I am going to tell you about the two verbs that express being in Spanish — **ser** and **estar.** Both verbs literally mean *to be,* but **ser** refers to the essence of being, such as the roundness of a ball, and **estar** refers to the changing nature of being, such as the location of the ball. By the end of this chapter, you'll know all the forms of **ser** and **estar** and when to use one or the other in a sentence.

Being is the most basic of actions, and the information about it in this chapter can be of utmost importance to you, so *be* attentive!

Capturing the Essence of One's Being with Ser

When you meet someone for the first time, you probably ask a series of questions to find out who that person is. You may ask that person about his or her profession, hometown, or relationship to others — is that person a son or daughter, a husband or wife, a father or mother? As you converse, the qualities of the person's personality may show through. He or she may appear sensitive or funny or interesting. All of these relatively unchanging qualities comprise a person's essence — the unchanging being of a person, place, or thing. Think of the verb **ser** as the *what-it-is* verb. When you need to tell somebody what something is, use the verb **ser.**

When expressing this form of *being* in Spanish, you use the verb **ser,** an irregular verb that has the following present-tense forms:

ser = to be	
soy	somos
eres	sois
es	son
Él **es** abogado. = He *is* a lawyer.	

Here are some examples of descriptive sentences using **ser**:

> **Ella es alta.** = She is tall.
>
> **Ellos son estudiantes.** = They are students.
>
> **La señora González es bonita.** = Mrs. González is pretty.
>
> **Yo soy de California.** = I am from California.
>
> **La escuela es nueva.** = The school is new.

Give the correct form of the verb **ser** that you'd use if the following people or things were the subjects of your sentences. Here's an example:

mi hermana = *es*

1. ella = _____

2. nosotros = _____

3. mis amigos = _____

4. Juan = _____

5. tú = _____

6. su padre = _____

7. el museo = _____

8. los niños = _____

9. Miguel y Elena = _____

10. ellos = _____

Being Here, There, or Anywhere with *Estar*

Certain aspects of one's being are variable. You may be sad one day and ecstatic the next. A friend may be ill. Your mother-in-law may be vacationing in Cancun. Those forms of being don't define a person's nature, but rather they define temporary conditions that typically are affected by outside influences.

When describing the changing nature of a person, place, or thing in Spanish, you use the verb **estar**. Like **ser**, **estar** literally translates as *to be,* but you typically use **estar** to describe more variable forms of being, such as health, feelings, and location. Like **ser**, **estar** is an irregular verb that takes the following present-tense forms:

estar = to be	
estoy	estamos
estás	estáis
está	están
Ellos **están** en el parque. = They *are* at the park.	

Because most forms of *being* have to do with temporary conditions, you can find plenty of uses for the verb **estar,** as the following examples illustrate:

Nosotros estamos en el cine. = We are at the cinema.

Ellos están aburridos. = They are bored.

Ella está triste. = She is sad.

Yo estoy enfermo. = I am sick.

Juan está en la playa. = Juan is at the beach.

Accents are used in four of the forms of **estar.** (Check out the conjugation chart earlier in the section.) Accent marks to show stress in Spanish are used when a word does not fall into one of the following categories:

✔ In words that end in a vowel or *n* or *s*, the stress naturally falls on the second-to-last syllable. In *mañana* (tomorrow), for example, the stress is on *-ña*.

✔ In words that end in a consonant other than *n* or *s*, the stress naturally falls on the last syllable. In the word *cantar* (to sing), you stress *-tar*.

Give the correct form of the verb **estar** that you'd use if the following people or things were the subjects of your sentences. Here's an example:

su casa = *está*

11. sus padres = _____

12. Emilio = _____

13. mis hermanas = _____

14. Francisco y Elena = _____

15. Juana y yo = _____

16. Uds. = _____

17. tú = _____

18. nosotros = _____

19. yo = _____

20. el edificio nuevo = _____

Choosing Your Manner of Being: Ser or Estar?

Perhaps the most difficult part about using **ser** and **estar** correctly in a sentence is choosing which one to use. The concept of two different types of being — unchanging essential being and being that changes depending on various conditions — is easy enough to grasp, but when you encounter different types of being, trying to pigeonhole them as one or the other can be quite challenging.

This section provides some additional guidelines that can help you decide whether to use **ser** or **estar**. The exercises in this section provide you with additional practice, mixing it up a little, so you not only need to know which form of the verb to use but also which verb is most appropriate. Be prepared to be challenged.

Deciding when to use ser

You already know that you use the verb **ser** to describe the unchanging characteristics of a person, place, or thing, but what exactly does that mean? The following lists provide additional details to help you identify situations in which to use **ser**:

Origin and Nationality

Ella es de España. = She is from Spain.

Ella es española. = She is Spanish.

The Four P's: Personality, Physical Attributes, Profession, and Possession

Él es divertido. = He is fun.

Susana es baja. = Susana is short.

Mi padre es un médico. = My father is a doctor.

El carro azul es mío. = The blue car is mine.

Date and Time

Hoy es el seis de enero. = Today is of January 6th.

Son las nueve de la noche. = It is 9 p.m.

Relationships

Ellos son mis padres. = They are my parents.

Rafael es mi mejor amigo. = Rafael is my best friend.

Deciding when to use estar

You know to use the verb **estar** to describe the changing characteristics of a person, place, or thing, but what exactly does that mean? The following list provides additional details to help you identify situations in which to use **estar**:

Location

Su casa está en la avenida Juárez. = Her house is on Juarez Avenue.

El cine está cerca del centro. = The cinema is near the center of town.

Mood and Physical Condition

El profesor está enojado. = The teacher is angry.

Mi madre está emocionada. = My mother is excited.

Los estudiantes están aburridos. = The students are bored.

La señorita Martínez está enferma. = Miss Martinez is sick.

Result of an Action

Los niños están de pie. = The children are standing.

La audiencia está sentada. = The audience is seated.

Translate the following sentences into Spanish. Choose whether you'd use **ser** or **estar** to express *to be*, based on the lists of uses for **ser** and **estar.** I show you how in the following example:

My mother is very tall. = *Mi madre es muy alta.*

Use the accent marks on the forms of estar when appropriate.

21. We are tired.

_____

22. They are very excited.

_____

23. The wedding is the 27th of June.

_____

24. The new student is from Germany.

_____

25. His father is a pilot.

_____

26. They are my grandparents.

_____

27. The new mall is near the river.

_____

28. Alma is very depressed today.

_____

29. The students in his class are very smart.

_____

30. David is (feeling) terrible.

_____

Answer Key

Give the correct form of **ser** that you'd use if the following people or things were the subjects of your sentences.

1. ella = *es*

2. nosotros = *somos*

3. mis amigos = *son*

4. Juan = *es*

5. tú = *eres*

6. su padre = *es*

7. el museo = *es*

8. los niños = *son*

9. Miguel y Elena = *son*

10. ellos = *son*

Give the correct form of **estar** that you'd use if the following people or things were the subjects of your sentences.

11. sus padres = *están*

12. Emilio = *está*

13. mis hermanas = *están*

14. Francisco y Elena = *están*

15. Juana y yo = *estamos*

16. Uds. = *están*

17. tú = *estás*

18. nosotros = *estamos*

19. yo = *estoy*

20. el edificio nuevo = *está*

Translate the following sentences into Spanish. Choose whether you'd use **ser** or **estar** to express *to be.*

21. We are tired.

Nosotros estamos cansados.

22. They are very excited.

    Ellos están muy emocionados.

23. The wedding is the 27th of June.

    La boda es el veintisiete de junio.

24. The new student is from Germany.

    El estudiante nuevo es de alemania.

25. His father is a pilot.

    Su padre es piloto.

26. They are my grandparents.

    Ellos son mis abuelos.

27. The new mall is near the river.

    El centro comercial nuevo está cerca del río.

28. Alma is very depressed today.

    Alma está muy deprimida hoy.

29. The students in his class are very smart.

    Los estudiantes en su clase son muy inteligentes.

30. David is (feeling) terrible.

    David está terrible.

Chapter 8

Wrestling with Some Irregular Formations

In This Chapter

▶ Meeting some common stem-changing verbs face-to-face

▶ Dealing with spelling changes in some verb conjugations

▶ Expanding your repertoire with the versatility of **hay**

▶ Talking about the weather with the verbs **hacer** and **estar**

*E*very language has its share of troublemakers — the exceptions to the rules. The most famous of these rules in the English language has to be: *i* before *e* except after *c* or when pronounced as *a* as in "neighbor" and "weigh." Spanish verbs have several exceptions that are likewise dedicated to flustering beginning Spanish speakers and writers. Some verbs insist on changing their verb stems depending on the conjugation. Others change their spellings.

This chapter introduces you to the mind-muddling, stem-changing, and spelling-changing verbs and lets you in on the tricks to conjugating them properly so that you can retain their proper pronunciations. You find out how to tap the power of the diminutive yet powerful verb **hay,** and you discover various ways to discuss the weather with the two primary forecasting verbs **hacer** and **estar.**

Getting a Grip on Stem-Changing Verbs

When you hear the term *stem-changing verbs,* you may imagine some weird grammatical creature in a sci-fi flick that morphs as terrified beginning Spanish students attempt to conjugate it. Dealing with stem-changing verbs is not exactly that bad, but it requires some patience and understanding. To help you cope, keep the following points in mind:

✔ Focus on present-tense conjugations for now. The chapters in Part IV deal with irregularities in other tenses.

✔ You encounter three types of stem-changing verbs in which the vowel used in the stem changes from *e* to *i, e* to *ie,* or *o* to *ue.*

✔ The verb **jugar** has a stem-change from *u* to *ue,* but it doesn't constitute its own category. I include it here, however, because it follows the same rules as other stem-changers.

✔ Stem changes occur in all of the present-tense forms of the verb *except* for the **nosotros** and the **vosotros** forms.

Sometimes the conjugation format for stem-changing verbs is referred to as the *boot,* because if you were to draw a dark line around the forms that have a stem change, they'd resemble a boot. Check out Figure 8-1 to see what I mean.

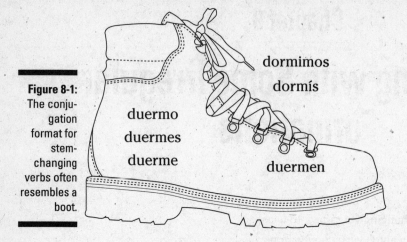

Figure 8-1:
The conjugation format for stem-changing verbs often resembles a boot.

dormimos

dormís

duermo

duermes

duerme

duermen

The following tables are examples of each type of stem-changing verb.

pedir (*e* to *i*) = to ask for	
pido	pedimos
pides	pedís
pide	piden
Uds. **piden.** = You (plural, formal) *ask for.*	

Other verbs in which the stem changes from *e* to *i* are in Table 8-1:

Table 8-1	Verbs with *e* to *i* Stem Changes
Verb	*Translation*
competir	to compete
despedirse	to say goodbye to
reírse	to laugh
repetir	to repeat
seguir	to follow
server	to serve
sonreírse	to smile
vestirse	to get dressed

perder (*e* to *ie*) = to lose	
pierdo	perdemos
pierdes	perdéis
pierde	pierden
Él **pierde.** = He *loses.*	

Other verbs in which the stem changes from *e* to *ie* include the verbs in Table 8-2:

Table 8-2	Verbs with *e* to *ie* Stem Changes
Verb	*Translation*
cerrar	to close
comenzar	to begin
despertarse	to wake up
empezar	to begin
merendar	to have a snack
nevar	to snow
pensar	to think
recomendar	to recommend
sentarse	to sit down

dormir (*o* to *ue*) = to sleep	
duermo	dormimos
duermes	dormís
duerme	duermen
Ellas **duermen.** = They (female) *sleep.*	

Table 8-3 shows other verbs in which the stem changes from *o* to *ue*:

Table 8-3	Verbs with *o* to *ue* Stem Changes
Verb	*Translation*
acostarse	to go to bed
almorzar	to eat lunch
contrar	to count
costar	to cost
encontrar	to find
mostrar	to show
recorder	to record
volar	to fly

The one and only verb in which the stem changes from *u* to *ue* is the verb **jugar.** Here is its conjugation:

jugar (*u* to *ue*) = to play a sport or a game	
juego	jugamos
juegas	jugáis
juega	juegan
Tú **juegas.** = You (familiar) *play*.	

Give the correct conjugated forms of the following stem-changing verbs based on the subjects given. This activity contains a mix of all three types of stem-changers — *e* to *i*, *e* to *ie*, and *o* to *ue* — so be careful.

Here's an example:

los niños/dormir = *los niños durmieron*

When using reflexive verbs, put the reflexive pronoun in front of the conjugated verb form. Also keep in mind that no stem-changes occur in the **nosotros** or the **vosotros** forms.

1. ellos/cerrar (ie) = _____

2. yo/probar (ue) = _____

3. Tomás/empezar (ie) = _____

4. nosotros/acostarse (ue) = _____

5. él/pedir (i) = _____

6. tú/dormir (ue) = _____

7. el profesor/mostrar (ue) = _____

8. ella/servir (i) = _____

9. nosotros/preferir (i) = _____

10. Pilar y Antonio/repetir (i) = _____

11. mis hermanos/vestirse (i) = _____

12. su tío/recordar (ue) = _____

13. yo/almorzar (ue) = _____

14. tú/pensar (ie) = _____

15. los libros/costar (ue) = _____

Presto Change-O: Verbs with Spelling Changes

Stem-changing verbs experience spelling changes that arise from the requirements of the conjugation. Other verbs require spelling changes based on pronunciation. Spanish is a phonetic language, so what you see is what you get. Or, more precisely, what you see is what you say or what you hear.

To keep pronunciation consistent, spelling changes are often required. As a verb is conjugated, changes in its spelling may alter the way the word is pronounced, so additional spelling changes are required to ensure that the resulting pronunciation of the word matches the pronunciation of the original. To provide some semblance of logic to these spelling changes, I've divided the spelling changes into these eight groups:

- ✔ **Group 1:** Soft *g* changes to *j* in front of an **-o** or an **-a** ending.

- ✔ **Group 2:** Hard *gu* changes to *g* in front of an **-o** or an **-a** ending.

- ✔ **Group 3:** Hard *qu* changes to *c* in front of an **-o** or an **-a** ending.

- ✔ **Group 4:** The *c* in *cer* or *cir* verbs, when preceded by a consonant, changes to a *z* in front of an **-o** or an **-a** ending.

- ✔ **Group 5:** The *c* in *cer* or *cir* verbs, when preceded by a vowel, changes to a *zc* in front of an **-o** or an **-a** ending. (This spelling-change rule is not dictated by pronunciation reasons, but it still falls under the category of a spelling change rule.)

- ✔ **Group 6:** Hard *c* changes to *qu* in front of an **-e** ending.

- ✔ **Group 7:** The letter *z* changes to *c* in front of an **-e** ending.

- ✔ **Group 8:** Hard *g* changes to *gu* in front of an **-e** ending.

Groups 6 through 8 don't affect the present tense, so you work with them in Part III of *Spanish Verbs For Dummies*, in which I cover the subjunctive mood. Following are examples of spelling changes in the present tense from the first five groups. Pay particular attention to the **yo** form, which has an **-o** ending.

Group 1 (soft *g* to *j*): escoger = to choose	
escojo	escogemos
escoges	escogéis
escoge	escogen
Uds. **escogen.** = You (plural, formal) *choose.*	

Another verb in this group is **proteger** (to protect).

Group 2 (hard *gu* to *g*): distinguir = to distinguish	
distingo	distinguimos
distingues	distinguís
distingue	distinguen
Ella **distingue.** = *She distinguishes.*	

Two other verbs in this group are **conseguir** (to attain) and **seguir** (to follow).

Group 3 (hard *qu* to *c*): delinquir = to offend	
delinco	delinquimos
delinques	delinquís
delinque	delinquen
Yo **delinco.** = I *offend.*	

This verb stands alone. I can't think of another verb that follows its example.

Group 4 (*c* to *z*): convencer = to convince	
convenzo	convencemos
convences	convencéis
convence	convencen
Vosotros **convencéis.** = You (plural, familiar) *convince*.	

Another verb in this group is **vencer** (to defeat, to conquer).

Group5 (*c* to *cz*): conocer = to know, to be familiar with	
conozco	conocemos
conoces	conocéis
conoce	conocen
Nosotras **conocemos.** = We (female) *know*.	

Other verbs in this group are **conducir** (to drive), **producir** (to produce), **traducir** (to translate), **crecer** (to grow), **ofrecer** (to offer), and **pertenecer** (to pertain).

Expressing Yourself with the Puny but Powerful Hay

The tiny verb **hay** packs a powerful punch in Spanish. Depending on the context in which you use it, this little three-letter word is a universal sentence starter that can take on any of the following meanings:

- ✔ There is . . .
- ✔ There are . . .
- ✔ Is there . . . ?
- ✔ Are there . . . ?

Take a look at just how versatile this mighty **hay** can be in the following examples:

Hay un libro en la mesa. = There is a book on the table.

Hay veinticinco estudiantes en la clase. = There are 25 students in the class.

¿Hay un libro en la mesa? = Is there a book on the table?

¿Hay veinticinco estudiantes en la clase? = Are there 25 students in the class?

Translate the following sentences into Spanish using the puny but powerful **hay.** Here's an example to get you started:

There are a lot of boys in the class. = *Hay muchos chicos en la clase.*

Be sure to add an upside down question mark at the beginning of any questions as well as the "regular" question mark at the end.

16. There are many books in the library.

   _____

17. There is a red car in front of the store.

   _____

18. Is there a television in the living room?

   _____

19. Are there many students in the school?

   _____

20. There is a cinema next to the supermarket.

   _____

Forecasting the Weather with *Hacer* and *Estar*

When you need to say something but really have nothing to say, you can always break the proverbial ice by talking about the weather. Discussing the weather in Spanish means using the verb **hacer,** which means *to do* or *to make*. Although it doesn't translate literally in weather expressions, **hacer** is used to mean *it is* or *it's*.

The examples that follow in Table 8-4 are some common weather expressions that use the verb **hacer:**

Table 8-4	Weather Expressions That Use *Hacer*
Phrase	*Translation*
Hace (mucho) calor.	It's (very) hot.
Hace (mucho) fresco.	It's (very) cool.
Hace (mucho) frío.	It's (very) cold.
Hace (mucho) sol.	It's (very) sunny.
Hace (mucho) viento.	It's (very) windy.
Hace (muy) buen tiempo.	It's (very) nice weather.
Hace (muy) mal tiempo.	It's (very) bad weather.

The verb **estar** (to be) also is used in weather expressions but to a much lesser degree (you can find out more about the versatile **estar** in Chapter 7). The following examples in Table 8-5 are weather descriptions that use **estar:**

Table 8-5	Weather Expressions That Use Estar
Phrase	*Translation*
Está lloviendo. (or **Llueve.**)	It's raining.
Está nevando. (or **Nieva.**)	It's snowing.
Está nublado.	It's cloudy.

The four seasons in Spanish are: **la primavera** (spring), **el verano** (summer), **el otoño** (fall), and **el invierno** (winter).

Answer *C* for *cierto* (true) or *F* for *falso* (false) to the following statements about the seasons and the weather, as I show you in the following example:

C Necesito un abrigo en el invierno en Minnesota. *(I need a coat in the winter in Minnesota.)*

21. _____ Hace buen tiempo en el verano.

22. _____ Hace mucho calor en el invierno.

23. _____ Está nublado mucho en el otoño.

24. _____ Me gusta mucho cuando hace buen tiempo.

25. _____ Hace mucho sol cuando está lloviendo.

26. _____ Nieva mucho en el verano.

27. _____ Voy a la playa cuando hace mucho frío.

28. _____ Necesito un suéter cuando hace fresco.

29. _____ Llueve mucho en los estados de Washington y Oregon.

30. _____ Hace viento mucho en la primavera.

Answer Key

Give the correct conjugated forms of the following stem-changing verbs based on the subjects given. I include a mixture of all three types of stem-changers in this activity — *e* to *i*, *e* to *ie*, and *o* to *ue* — so be careful.

1. ellos/cerrar (ie) = *cierran*

2. yo/probar (ue) = *pruebo*

3. Tomás/empezar (ie) = *empieza*

4. nosotros/acostarse (ue) = *nos acostamos*

5. él/pedir (i) = *pide*

6. tú/dormir (ue) = *duermes*

7. el profesor/mostrar (ue) = *muestra*

8. ella/servir (i) = *sirve*

9. nosotros/preferir (i) = *preferimos*

10. Pilar y Antonio/repetir (i) = *repiten*

11. mis hermanos/vestirse (i) = *se visten*

12. su tío/recordar (ue) = *recuerda*

13. yo/almorzar (ue) = *almuerzo*

14. tú/pensar (ie) = *piensas*

15. los libros/costar (ue) = *cuestan*

Translate the following sentences into Spanish using the puny but powerful **hay.**

16. There are many books in the library.

    Hay muchos libros en la biblioteca.

17. There is a red car in front of the store.

    Hay un carro rojo enfrente de la tienda.

18. Is there a television in the living room?

    ¿Hay un televisor en la sala?

19. Are there many students in the school?

    ¿Hay muchos estudiantes en la escuela?

20. There is a cinema next to the supermarket.

    Hay un cine al lado del supermercado.

    Answer *C* for *cierto* (true) or *F* for *falso* (false) to the following statements about the seasons and the weather.

21. *C* Hace buen tiempo en el verano. *(It's good weather in the summer.)*

22. *F* Hace mucho calor en el invierno. *(It's very hot in the winter.)*

23. *C* Está nublado mucho en el otoño. *(It's cloudy a lot in the fall.)*

24. *C* Me gusta mucho cuando hace buen tiempo. *(I like it a lot when the weather is nice.)*

25. *F* Hace mucho sol cuando está lloviendo. *(It's really sunny when it's raining.)*

26. *F* Nieva mucho en el verano. *(It snows a lot in the summer.)*

27. *F* Voy a la playa cuando hace mucho frío. *(I go to the beach when it's really cold.)*

28. *C* Necesito un suéter cuando hace fresco. *(I need a sweater when it's cool.)*

29. *C* Llueve mucho en los estados de Washington y Oregon. *(It rains a lot in the states of Washington and Oregon.)*

30. *C* Hace mucho viento en la primavera. *(It's really windy in the spring.)*

Part III
Working Out with the Remaining Simple Tenses

The 5th Wave   By Rich Tennant

"Here's an idea, let's practice conjugating verbs in Spanish. Last night, you were 'viviste la vida loca.' But this morning, you are 'viviendo la vida Pepto Bismol.'"

In this part . . .

The present tense can carry you only so far. You need other tenses and other moods to discuss past events and future occasions and to express your hopes, desires, and attitudes. The chapters in this part depart from the present but stick with the regular verbs. Here you find out how to describe past events in the preterit and imperfect, dream about upcoming prospects with the future tense, form conditional *what if* statements, and use the subjunctive mood to convey uncertainty about the present and past and express wishes, doubts, and opinions.

Each chapter provides a quick review of how to conjugate regular verbs in the specified tense or mood and helps you identify situations in which you should use the tense or mood.

Chapter 9

Looking Back with the Preterit and Imperfect Tenses

*W*hat's past is past. Or is it? The past tense can be a little murky in Spanish (and in English). Sometimes, an action in the past is complete: It's done, over, you can stick a fork in it. In other cases, past action is a little more vague. It doesn't relate to a specific event but to a past action that was continuous, ongoing, or habitual — something you "used to do" or "were doing," for example, at no set period or time. In English, you probably distinguish between these subtle nuances in past tense all the time without ever giving it a second thought, but to be able to effectively understand and use the different tenses in Spanish, you need to become much more aware of their differences.

In this chapter, you discover how to conjugate verbs in both the preterit and imperfect tenses, and you explore distinctions in usage. You encounter each tense separately and get plenty of practice with their respective conjugations. After you practice with each tense on its own, I mix it up a bit, challenging you to select the appropriate tense based on how each verb is used in a series of sample sentences.

Getting Over It with the Preterit

The *preterit tense* enables you to put the past behind you. It describes a completed past action — something that happened yesterday, last night, last week, last year, or at some other definite point in time. The action may have occurred a specific number of times or within an enclosed period of time, but it's done, finished. You have closure.

When working with the preterit, it helps to have some time words at your disposal, so you can describe, specifically, when a particular action took place. Table 9-1 lists time words commonly used with the preterit tense.

Table 9-1	Words That Describe Completed Actions
Term	**Translation**
ayer	yesterday
anteayer	day before yesterday
la semana pasada	last week
el mes pasado	last month
el año pasado	last year
esta mañana	this morning
esta tarde	this afternoon
anoche	last night
hace — dos días	two days — ago

To form regular **-ar** verbs in the preterit tense, you add the following endings to the verb stem:

yo -é	nosotros/as -amos
tú -aste	vosotros/as -asteis
él, ella -o Ud.	ellos/as -aron Uds.

So here's what the verb **hablar** looks like in the preterit tense:

hablar = to speak	
hablé	**hablamos**
hablaste	**hablasteis**
habló	**hablaron**
Yo **hablé.** = I *spoke.*	

Spelling changes, like the ones I discuss in Chapter 8, play a part in the preterit tense for some **-ar** verbs. Keep the following spelling changes in mind:

✔ **Change *z* to *c* in front of -é.**

    empezar (to begin) becomes **yo empecé**

✔ **Change hard *c* to *qu* in front of -é.**

    explicar (to explain) becomes **yo expliqué**

✔ **Change hard *g* to *gu* in front of -é.**

    llegar (to arrive) becomes **yo llegué**

To form regular **-er** and **-ir** verbs in the preterit tense, you add the following endings to the verb stem:

yo -í	nosotros/as -imos
tú -iste	vosotros/as -isteis
él, ella -ió Ud.	ellos/as -ieron Uds.

Here's what the verb **comer** looks like in the preterit tense:

comer = to eat	
comí	comimos
comiste	comisteis
comió	comieron
Él **comió.** = He *ate*.	

And here's what the verb **vivir** looks like in the preterit tense:

vivir = to live	
viví	vivimos
viviste	vivisteis
vivió	vivieron
Tú **viviste.** = You (familiar) *lived*.	

Notice that the **nosotros** forms of **-ar** and **-ir** verbs are the same in the preterit tense as they are in the present tense.

Put the following regular verbs into their correct preterit form according to the subjects given, as I show you here:

mi mamá/hablar = *mi mamá habló*

1. tú/escribir = _____

2. yo/correr = _____

3. ella/trabajar = _____

4. Tomás/comprar = _____

5. el niño/beber = _____

6. él/estudiar = _____

7. mi padre/abrir = _____

8. los estudiantes/andar = _____

9. nosotros/asistir = _____

10. ellos/vender = _____

Practicing with the Regular Preterit

Being able to use the preterit after learning how to form it often requires some additional practice. The key concept to wrap your brain around when it comes to the preterit tense is that the action is *completed in the past and shows no signs of continuing.* If you're looking to communicate this sense of finality, then the preterit is the tense for you.

Here's how I can use the preterit to describe a typical morning, from the time I woke up to the time I arrived at work (all completed actions):

Me levanté a las siete y media. = I woke up at 7:30.

Me duché. = I took a shower.

Me cepillé los dientes y me peiné. = I brushed my teeth and combed my hair.

Me vestí. = I got dressed.

Desayuné. = I ate breakfast.

Salí de la casa a las ocho y media. = I left home at 8:30.

Llegué a mi trabajo a las nueve. = I arrived at work at 9.

I could go on, but the monotony of my day would only make you sleepy. To keep things interesting, try your hand at it.

Translate the following statements into Spanish. Follow my lead:

My brother attended a concert last night. = *Mi hermano asistió a un concierto anoche.*

11. I ate at a Mexican restaurant yesterday.

_____

12. The plane arrived at 12:30 p.m.

_____

13. They left the day before yesterday.

_____

14. She washed the dishes last night.

_____

15. We cleaned the house last weekend.

_____

Answer *Sí* or *No* to the following preterit tense statements based on your past actions, as I show you in the following example:

Sí ¿Compraste un carro nuevo el año pasado? *(Did you buy a new car last year?)*

16. _____ ¿Llamaste a un amigo por teléfono ayer?

17. _____ ¿Visitaste a un museo el fin de semana pasado?

18. _____ ¿Hablaste con tu padre anteayer?

19. _____ ¿Limpiaste tu cuarto la semana pasada?

20. _____ ¿Lavaste los platos anoche?

21. _____ ¿Preparaste la cena anoche?

22. _____ ¿Corriste en el parque el mes pasado?

23. _____ ¿Miraste la televisión anoche?

24. _____ ¿Caminaste al centro esta mañana?

25. _____ ¿Comiste pizza esta tarde?

Giving Hazy Details with the Imperfect

The imperfect tense is vague and imprecise. That's why it's called *imperfect*. When you know something happened in the past, but you're not really sure when or how often, you use the *imperfect tense*. In English, you typically use the expressions *used to* or *always* to describe these actions:

I used to golf every Sunday.

My mom always made tamales for the holidays.

Chico used to run five miles a day.

The imperfect is used to describe continuous, ongoing, or habitual past action.

When forming the regular imperfect tense of **-ar** verbs, you add the following endings to the verb stem:

Yo -aba	nosotros/as -ábamos
Tú -abas	vosotros/as -abais
él, ella -aba Ud.	ellos/as -aban Ud.

So the imperfect conjugations of **hablar** are

hablar = to speak	
hablaba	hablábamos
hablabas	hablabais
hablaba	hablaban
Yo **hablaba.** = I *used to speak.*	

To conjugate **-er** and **-ir** regular verbs into the imperfect tense, you add the following endings to the verb stem:

yo –ía	nosotros/as -íamos
tú –ías	vosotros/as -íais
él, ella -ía Ud.	ellos/as -ían Uds.

So the imperfect conjugations of the verb **comer** are

comer = to eat	
comía	comíamos
comías	comíais
comía	comían
Nosotros **comíamos.** = We *used to eat.*	

And the imperfect conjugations of the verb **vivir** are

vivir = to live	
vivía	vivíamos
vivías	vivíais
vivía	vivían
Ud. **vivía.** = You (formal) *used to live.*	

Now that you have all of the regular imperfect conjugations, take a few minutes to etch it on your brain cells by practicing what you've learned.

Put the following verbs into their correct imperfect conjugations based on the subjects provided, as I demonstrate here:

tú/cocinar = *tú cocinabas*

26. María/comer = _____

27. ellos/cantar = _____

28. yo/asistir = _____

29. nosotros/andar = _____

30. tú/hablar = _____

31. mi madre/hacer = _____

32. ella/trabajar = _____

33. el profesor/abrir = _____

34. Juan y Raúl/vender = _____

35. Uds./leer = _____

Practicing with the Regular Imperfect

You know the regular imperfect conjugations and can recite them in your sleep, but can you use them in a sentence? You're about to find out. In this section, you get to test your skills with the regular imperfect, but first, see Table 9-2 to review the list of time expressions that are commonly used with the imperfect tense:

Table 9-2	Words That Describe Ongoing or Habitual Action
Term	*Translation*
siempre	always
todos los fines de semana	every weekend
todos los días	every day
los lunes	on Mondays
los martes	on Tuesdays
los miércoles	on Wednesdays
los jueves	on Thursdays
los viernes	on Fridays
los sábados	on Saturdays
los domingos	on Sundays

The imperfect is a very useful past tense for expressing background actions or actions that were going on when they were suddenly interrupted by a preterit tense action. The actions described by the imperfect tense are ongoing or habitual past actions that don't show their beginning or their end or any particular time limitations.

Translate the following sentences into Spanish using the imperfect tense. Here's an example to get you started:

I used to attend church every Sunday. = *Yo asistía a la iglesia todos los domingos.*

36. I used to run in the park on Saturdays.

_____

37. My father used to work for G.M.

_____

38. We used to study together every weekend.

_____

39. The students read the newspaper in class every day.

_____

40. My mother always prepared tacos on Sunday.

_____

41. The children used to visit the museum every week.

_____

42. I used to read the newspaper every morning.

_____

43. They always talked on the phone on Friday evening.

_____

44. She used to travel to Europe every summer.

_____

45. Pedro used to get up early every day.

_____

PRACTICE

Answer *Sí* or *No* to the following statements based on your past actions. Because these statements are in the imperfect tense, they refer to activities that you *used to* do. Here's an example:

Sí ¿Jugabas al tenis? *(Did you used to play tennis?)*

46. _____ ¿Trabajabas mucho?

47. _____ ¿Estudiabas con amigos los fines de semana?

48. _____ ¿Leías el periódico todos los días?

49. _____ ¿Preparabas la cena para la familia?

50. _____ ¿Te levantabas temprano los fines de semana?

51. _____ ¿Mirabas la televisión mucho?

52. _____ ¿Corrías en el parque los fines de semana?

53. _____ ¿Visitabas a un museo mucho?

54. _____ ¿Hablabas con tus padres por teléfono mucho?

55. _____ ¿Descansabas mucho los fines de semana?

Preterit or Imperfect? You Decide

Now, the moment you've been waiting for — the moment that challenges you to select the right tense for the right job. You're given a sentence that expresses or describes an action from the past, and it's up to you to decide which tense to use — preterit or imperfect. When choosing between the two, review the uses for the preterit and the imperfect in Table 9-3.

Table 9-3	Uses of the Preterit and Imperfect Tenses
Uses of the preterit	*Uses of the imperfect*
To describe an action or a series of actions which were completed in the past	To describe ongoing or continuous past actions, without focusing on their beginning or end
To express an action, event, or state of mind that happened in the past and was completed at a specific moment or period	To describe conditions in the past
	To tell the time in the past

When choosing between the imperfect and the preterit, watch for time words to use as clues, and remember that the imperfect often translates to English as "used to."

After you've decided on the appropriate tense, you can then conjugate the verb and supply any necessary time phrases to complete the translation. The following practice activities can help you see for yourself whether you've grasped the difference between these two past tenses. After you've figured it out, you may just find yourself saying, **"¡Viva la diferencia!"**

Translate the following sentences into Spanish. You must choose which past tense to use — the preterit or the imperfect — and then conjugate the verb accordingly, as I show you here:

I wrote a letter to my sister last night. = *Yo escribí una carta a mi hermana anoche.*

56. The students at the private school wore uniforms.

_____

57. Juan didn't work last week.

_____

58. We always ate pizza on Fridays.

_____

59. She traveled to Europe last summer.

_____

60. My dad washed the dishes last night.

_____

61. The teacher used to talk in Spanish all of the time.

_____

62. Patricia and Jorge prepared a delicious dinner last weekend.

_____

63. Nico always celebrated his birthday in Mexico.

_____

64. He helped the children with their homework yesterday.

_____

65. My friends always practiced sports after school.

_____

Answer Key

Put the following regular verbs into their correct preterit form according to the subjects given.

1. tú/escribir = *escribiste*

2. yo/correr = *corrí*

3. ella/trabajar = *trabajó*

4. Tomás/comprar = *compró*

5. el niño/beber = *bebió*

6. él/estudiar = *estudió*

7. mi padre/abrir = *abrió*

8. los estudiantes/andar = *andaron*

9. nosotros/asistir = *asistimos*

10. ellos/vender = *vendieron*

Translate the following statements into Spanish.

11. I ate at a Mexican restaurant yesterday.

    Yo comí en un restaurante mexicano ayer.

12. The plane arrived at 12:30 p.m.

    El avión llegó a las doce y media.

13. They left the day before yesterday.

    Ellos salieron anteayer.

14. She washed the dishes last night.

    Ella lavó los platos anoche.

15. We cleaned the house last weekend.

    Nosotros limpiamos la casa el fin de semana pasado.

Answer *Sí* or *No* to the following preterit tense statements based on your past actions. Because the answers are based on your own experience, there are no right or wrong answers, but I have provided the English translations for each question to help you check your own answers.

16. *Sí/No* ¿Llamaste a un amigo por teléfono ayer? *(Did you call a friend on the phone yesterday?)*

17. *Sí/No* ¿Visitaste a un museo el fin de semana pasado? *(Did you visit a museum last weekend?)*

18. *Sí/No* ¿Hablaste con tu padre anteayer? *(Did you talk with your father the day before yesterday?)*

19. *Sí/No* ¿Limpiaste tu cuarto la semana pasada? *(Did you clean your room last week?)*

20. *Sí/No* ¿Lavaste los platos anoche? *(Did you wash the dishes last night?)*

21. *Sí/No* ¿Preparaste la cena anoche? *(Did you prepare dinner last night?)*

22. *Sí/No* ¿Corriste en el parque el mes pasado? *(Did you run in the park last month?)*

23. *Sí/No* ¿Miraste la televisión anoche? *(Did you watch television last night?)*

24. *Sí/No* ¿Caminaste al centro esta mañana? *(Did you walk downtown this morning?)*

25. *Sí/No* ¿Comiste pizza esta tarde? *(Did you eat pizza this afternoon?)*

Put the following verbs into their correct imperfect conjugations based on the subjects given.

26. María/comer = *comía*

27. ellos/cantar = *cantaban*

28. yo/asistir = *asistía*

29. nosotros/andar = *andábamos*

30. tú/hablar = *hablabas*

31. mi madre/hacer = *hacía*

32. ella/trabajar = *trabajaba*

33. el profesor/abrir = *abría*

34. Juan y Raúl/vender = *vendían*

35. Uds./leer = *leían*

Translate the following sentences into Spanish using the imperfect tense.

36. I used to run in the park on Saturdays.

Yo corría en el parque los sábados.

37. My father used to work for G.M.

Mi padre trabajaba para G.M.

38. We used to study together every weekend.

Nosotros estudiábamos juntos todos los fines de semana.

39. The students read the newspaper in class every day.

Los estudiantes leían el periódico en clase todos los días.

40. My mother always prepared tacos on Sunday.

Mi madre siempre preparaba tacos los domingos.

41. The children used to visit the museum every week.

     Los niños visitaban el museo cada semana.

42. I used to read the newspaper every morning.

     Yo leía el periódico cada mañana.

43. They always talked on the phone on Friday evening.

     Ellos siempre hablaban por teléfono los viernes por la noche.

44. She used to travel to Europe every summer.

     Ella viajaba a Europa cada verano.

45. Pedro used to get up early every day.

     Pedro se levantaba temprano todos los días.

     Answer *Sí* or *No* to the following statements based on your past actions. Because the answers are based on your own experience, there are no right or wrong answers, but I have provided the English translations for each question to help you check your own answers.

46. *Sí/No* ¿Trabajabas mucho? *(Did you used to work a lot?)*

47. *Sí/No* ¿Estudiabas con amigos los fines de semana? *(Did you used to study with friends on the week-end?)*

48. *Sí/No* ¿Leías el periódico todos los días? *(Did you used to read the newspaper every day?)*

49. *Sí/No* ¿Preparabas la cena para la familia? *(Did you used to prepare dinner for your family?)*

50. *Sí/No* ¿Te levantabas temprano los fines de semana? *(Did you used to get up early on the weekend?)*

51. *Sí/No* ¿Mirabas la televisión mucho? *(Did you used to watch television a lot?)*

52. *Sí/No* ¿Corrías en el parque los fines de semana? *(Did you used to run in the park on the weekend?)*

53. *Sí/No* ¿Visitabas a un museo mucho? *(Did you used to visit a museum a lot?)*

54. *Sí/No* ¿Hablabas con tus padres por teléfono mucho? *(Did you used to talk to your parents on the tele-phone a lot?)*

55. *Sí/No* ¿Descansabas mucho los fines de semana? *(Did you used to rest a lot on the weekends?)*

     Translate the following sentences into Spanish. You must choose which past tense to use — the preterit or the imperfect — and then conjugate the verb accordingly.

56. The students at the private school wore uniforms.

     Los estudiantes en la escuela privada llevaban uniformes.

57. Juan didn't work last week.

     Juan no trabajó la semana pasada?

58. We always ate pizza on Fridays.

Nosotros siempre comíamos pizza los viernes.

59. She traveled to Europe last summer.

Ella viajó a Europa el verano pasado.

60. My dad washed the dishes last night.

Mi papá lavó los platos anoche.

61. The teacher used to talk in Spanish all of the time.

La profesora siempre hablaba en español.

62. Patricia and Jorge prepared a delicious dinner last weekend.

Patricia y Jorge prepararon una cena deliciosa el fin de semana pasado.

63. Nico always celebrated his birthday in Mexico.

Nico siempre celebraba su cumpleaños en México.

64. He helped the children with their homework yesterday.

Él ayudó a los niños con su tarea ayer.

65. My friends always practiced sports after school.

Mis amigos siempre practicaban los deportes después de la escuela.

Chapter 10

Looking Ahead with the Future Tense

● ●

In This Chapter

▶ Conjugating regular forms of the future tense

▶ Understanding the uses of future tense

▶ Expressing yourself in future tense

● ●

Some people get tense about the future, because it's unknown and uncertain. When you're studying a foreign language, however, you may get tense about the future for entirely different reasons — perhaps because you don't know how to form the future tense or use it to describe future events or actions. This chapter builds your confidence by showing you the basics of forming and using the future tense to describe actions and events that *will* occur. When will they occur? Whenever you say they will, by using adverbs and adverbial phrases such as *tomorrow, next week, next year, this Saturday,* and *next month.* In this chapter, you discover the basics of forming the regular future tense and using adverbs to make your expressions more precise.

Forming the Regular Future Tense

The regular future tense is one of the easiest tenses to form. You simply take the entire **-ar, -er,** or **-ir** verb in its infinitive form and add the appropriate ending.

yo -é	nosotros/as -emos
tú -ás	vosotros/as -éis
él, ella -á Ud.	ellos/as -án Uds.

Here are examples of regular **-ar, -er,** and **-ir** verbs conjugated in the future tense, with a sentence given to show their use.

hablar = to speak	
hablaré	hablaremos
hablarás	hablaréis
hablará	hablarán
Tomás **hablará** por teléfono con Susana mañana. = Thomas *will talk* on the phone with Susan tomorrow.	

comer = to eat	
comeré	comeremos
comerás	comeréis
comerá	comerán
Nosotros **comeremos** pizza esta tarde. = We *will eat* pizza this afternoon.	

escribir = to write	
escribiré	escribiremos
escribirás	escribiréis
escribirá	escribirán
Ella **escribirá** una carta mañana. = She *will write* a letter tomorrow.	

Translate each phrase, giving the correct subject pronoun for the following future tense verbs. (Remember that in some forms more than one choice is correct.) Here's what I mean:

tú llevarás = *you will wear*

1. _____ venderé = _____

2. _____ comprará = _____

3. _____ celebraremos = _____

4. _____ ganará = _____

5. _____ vivirás = _____

6. _____ bailarán = _____

7. _____ cantaré = _____

8. _____ comeremos = _____

9. _____ hablará = _____

10. _____ llamarás = _____

Put the following infinitives in the correct future form according to the subject given. The subject may be a name, a noun, or a pronoun. Remember, all future tense conjugated forms have a written accent mark *except* the nosotros form.

Here's an example:

ella/ir de compras = *irá de compras*

11. José/pintar = _____

12. Raúl y Susana/bailar = _____

13. El profesor/acercarse = _____

14. Mi papá/visitar = _____

15. Mis amigos/estudiar = _____

16. Yo/ganar = _____

17. Ellos/aprender = _____

18. Nosotros/jugar = _____

19. El mecánico/reparar = _____

20. Tú/cerrar = _____

Talking About the Future

Now that you have become successful at forming the regular future tense, you get a chance to put what you've learned into practice by describing future actions in complete sentences. Table 10-1 gives a list of some useful time expressions that give more specific information to your audience as to when in the future the action will take place.

Table 10-1	Words That Describe Future Action
Term	*Translation*
mañana	tomorrow
mañana por la mañana	tomorrow morning
mañana por la tarde	tomorrow afternoon
mañana por la noche	tomorrow night
el sábado que viene	next Saturday
la semana que viene	next week
el mes que viene	next month
el año que viene	next year
más tarde	later
esta tarde	this afternoon
esta noche	tonight

When conjugating reflexive verbs in the future tense, the reflexive pronoun goes in front of the conjugated verb form (see Chapter 3 for more on reflexive verbs).

Translate the following future tense sentences into Spanish, as I show you here:

I will go shopping tomorrow. = *Yo iré de compras mañana.*

21. Susana will clean her room tomorrow.

_____

22. The boys will play soccer later.

_____

23. My parents will travel to Europe this summer.

_____

24. I will prepare dinner at 6 p.m.

_____

25. We will call the office next week.

_____

26. Rafael will sing at the wedding this summer.

_____

27. They will wake up at 8 a.m. tomorrow.

_____

28. You (familiar sing.) will watch TV this afternoon. Right?

_____

29. I will study with Miguel for the math exam.

_____

30. José and María will run in the park this weekend.

_____

Answer *C* for *cierto* (true) or *F* for *falso* (false) to the following future tense sentences, based on what you will be doing in the future. Here's an example:

C Almorzaré a la una hoy. (*I will eat lunch at 1 p.m. today.*)

You can omit the subject pronoun in a Spanish sentence if the subject is clear. For example: if the verb ending is **-é** in the future tense, the subject clearly is **yo.**

31. _____ Cantaré en el coro este domingo.

32. _____ Iré de compras mañana.

33. _____ Miraré la televisión esta noche.

34. _____ Compraré un traje de baño nuevo este verano.

35. _____ Visitaré a Europa en las vacaciones de primavera.

36. _____ Me acostaré a las once esta noche.

37. _____ Prepararé una sopa para la cena hoy.

38. _____ Hablaré por teléfono con mi mamá este fin de semana.

39. _____ Me despertaré a las 6:00 mañana por la mañana.

40. _____ Estudiaré el español por dos horas todos los días.

Answer the following questions with complete sentences. Note that all sentences refer to future actions.

In Spanish, you can omit the subject if the subject is clear. Therefore, you can omit **yo** in these answers. Likewise, in Spanish, two negatives do not equal a positive; in fact, you must use two no's to respond negatively in Spanish. The equivalent in English takes the form, "No, I won't be eating . . ."

Here's how your answers might look:

¿Correrás en el parque mañana? *(Will you run in the park tomorrow?)*

Positive response: *Sí, yo correré en el parque mañana.*

Negative response: *No, yo no correré en el parque mañana.*

41. ¿Comerás pizza con tus amigos este fin de semana?

_____

42. ¿Hablarás con tus padres por teléfono mañana?

_____

43. ¿Recibirás un millón de dólares?

_____

44. ¿Trabajarás mucho el año que viene?

_____

45. ¿Comprarás un carro nuevo el mes que viene?

_____

46. ¿Comprenderás el español mejor en el futuro?

_____

47. ¿Te levantarás temprano mañana?

_____

48. ¿Leerás el periódico mañana por la mañana?

_____

49. ¿Jugarás el fútbol este fin de semana?

_____

50. ¿Limpiarás la casa esta tarde?

_____

PRACTICE

Answer the following future tense questions as indicated. I show you how here:

¿Volverá Juan de su vacación hoy? = No, *Juan no volverá de su vacación hoy.*

Note: Feel free to replace names with pronouns where appropriate.

51. ¿Trabajará el Sr. Gómez mañana?

Sí, _____

52. ¿Visitarán los estudiantes a Europa este verano?

No, _____

53. ¿Calificará la profesora los papeles esta tarde?

Sí, _____

54. ¿Llamará tu mamá por teléfono hoy?

No, _____

55. ¿Escucharás la radio este fin de semana?

Sí, _____

56. ¿Preparará tu mamá la cena esta noche?

Sí, _____

57. ¿Ganará el equipo el partido de fútbol?

No, _____

58. ¿Lavarán los niños los platos esta noche?

Sí, _____

59. ¿Gastará Felipe mucho dinero el año que viene?

No, _____

60. ¿Mirarán los estudiantes una película mañana?

Sí, _____

Answer Key

Give a correct subject pronoun for the following future tense verbs. (Remember that in some forms more than one choice is correct.) Then give the definition.

1. *yo* venderé = *I will sell*

2. *él, ella, or Ud.* comprará = *he, she, or you (formal) will buy*

3. *nosotros/as* celebraremos = *we will celebrate*

4. *él, ella, or Ud.* ganará = *he, she or you (formal) will win or earn*

5. *tú* vivirás = *you will live*

6. *ellos or Uds.* bailarán = *they or you (plural) will dance*

7. *yo* cantaré = *I will sing*

8. *nosotros* comeremos = *we will eat*

9. *él, ella, or Ud.* hablará = *he, she, or you will speak*

10. *tú* llamarás = *you will call*

Put the following infinitives in the correct future form according to the subject given.

11. José/pintar = *pintará*

12. Raúl y Susana/bailar = *bailarán*

13. El profesor/acercar = *acercará*

14. Mi papá/visitar = *visitará*

15. Mis amigos/estudiar = *estudiarán*

16. Yo/ganar = *ganaré*

17. Ellos/aprender = *aprenderán*

18. Nosotros/jugar = *jugaremos*

19. El mecánico/reparar = *reparará*

20. Tú/cerrar = *cerrarás*

Translate the following future tense sentences into Spanish.

21. Susana will clean her room tomorrow.

    Susana liampiará su cuarto mañana.

22. The boys will play soccer later.

    Los muchachos jugarán el fútbol más tarde.

23. My parents will travel to Europe this summer.

    Mis padres viajarán a Europa este verano.

24. I will prepare dinner at 6 p.m.

    Yo prepararé la cena a las seis.

25. We will call the office next week.

    Nosotros llamaremos a la oficina la semana que viene.

26. Rafael will sing at the wedding this summer.

    Rafael cantará en la boda este verano.

27. They will wake up at 8 a.m. tomorrow.

    Ellos se despertarán a las ocho mañana.

28. You (familiar) will watch T.V. this afternoon. Right?

    Tú mirarás la televisión esta tarde. ¿Verdad?

29. I will study with Miguel for the math exam.

    Yo estudiaré con Miguel para el examen de matemáticas.

30. José and María will run in the park this weekend.

    José y María correrán en el parque este fin de semana.

    The following *C* for *cierto* (true) or *F* for *falso* (false) answers are purely subjective. I have given the English translations and from that information you can surmise whether you should have answered cierto or falso.

31. *C/F* Cantaré en el coro este domingo. *(I will sing in the choir this Sunday.)*

32. *C/F* Iré de compras mañana. *(I will go shopping tomorrow.)*

33. *C/F* Miraré la televisión esta noche. *(I will watch TV tonight.)*

34. *C/F* Compraré un traje de baño nuevo este verano. *(I will buy a new swimsuit this summer.)*

35. *C/F* Visitaré a Europa en las vacaciones de primavera. *(I will visit Europe during Spring Break.)*

36. C/F Me acostaré a las once esta noche. (I will go to bed at 11 o'clock tonight.)

37. *C/F* Prepararé una sopa para la cena hoy. *(I will prepare soup for dinner today.)*

38. C/F Hablaré por teléfono con mi mamá este fin de semana. (I will talk on the telephone with my mom this weekend.)

39. *C/F* Me despertaré a las 6:00 mañana por la mañana. *(I will wake-up at 6 o'clock tomorrow morning.)*

40. *C/F* Estudiaré el español por dos horas todos los días. *(I will study Spanish for two hours every day.)*

The following questions also are subjective, and they are written in the yes/no question style. To assess your answers, read through the translations. If you have a negative response, replace the sí with the two no's in parentheses.

41. ¿Comerás pizza con tus amigos este fin de semana? *(Will you eat pizza with your friends this weekend?)*

   Sí (No), yo (no) comeré pizza con mis amigos este fin de semana.

42. ¿Hablarás con tus padres por teléfono mañana? *(Will you speak with your parents on the telephone tomorrow?)*

   Sí (No), yo (no) hablaré con mis padres por teléfono mañana.

43. ¿Recibirás un millón de dólares? *(Will you receive a million dollars?)*

   Sí (No), yo (no) recibiré un millón de dólares.

44. ¿Trabajarás mucho el año que viene? *(Will you work a lot next year?)*

   Sí (No), yo (no) trabajaré mucho el año que viene.

45. ¿Comprarás un carro nuevo el mes que viene? *(Will you buy a new car next month?)*

   Sí (No), yo (no) compraré un carro nuevo el mes que viene.

46. ¿Comprenderás el español mejor en el futuro? *(Will you understand Spanish better in the future?)*

   Sí (No), yo (no) comprenderé el español mejor en el futuro.

47. ¿Te levantarás temprano mañana? *(Will you get up early tomorrow?)*

   Sí (No), yo (no) me levantaré temprano mañana.

48. ¿Leerás el periódico mañana por la mañana? *(Will you read the newspaper tomorrow morning?)*

   Sí (No), yo (no) leeré el periódico mañana por la mañana.

49. ¿Jugarás el fútbol este fin de semana? *(Will you play soccer this weekend?)*

   Sí (No), yo (no) jugaré el fútbol este fin de semana.

50. ¿Limpiarás la casa esta tarde? *(Will you clean the house this afternoon?)*

   Sí (No), yo (no) limpiaré la casa esta tarde.

The last ten activities are simple yes/no questions that you answer as indicated. The answers include subjects as they appear in the question. Keep in mind, however, that you can change a name to a pronoun *or* leave it out entirely, because the person being spoken about is clear.

51. ¿Trabajará el Sr. Gómez mañana?

   Sí, el Sr. Gómez trabajará mañana.

52. ¿Visitarán los estudiantes a Europa este verano?

No, *los estudiantes no visitarán a Europa este verano.*

53. ¿Calificará la profesora los papeles esta tarde?

Sí, *la profesora calificará los papeles esta tarde.*

54. ¿Llamará tu mamá por teléfono hoy?

No, *mi mamá no llamará por teléfono hoy.*

55. ¿Escucharás la radio este fin de semana?

Sí, *escucharé la radio este fin de semana.*

56. ¿Preparará tu mamá la cena esta noche?

Sí, *mi mamá preparará la cena esta noche.*

57. ¿Ganará el equipo el partido de fútbol?

No, *el equipo no ganará el partido de fútbol.*

58. ¿Lavarán los niños los platos esta noche?

Sí, *los niños lavarán los platos esta noche.*

59. ¿Gastará Felipe mucho dinero el año que viene?

No, *Felipe no gastará mucho dinero el año que viene.*

60. ¿Mirarán los estudiantes una película mañana?

Sí, *los estudiantes mirarán una película mañana.*

Chapter 11

Mastering the Big *If* with the Conditional Tense

In This Chapter

▶ Making actions conditional

▶ Knowing when to use the conditional tense

▶ Putting the conditional tense to work . . . on one condition

*S*hould've, could've, would've . . . that's what the conditional tense is all about. If the conditions were appropriate, then the action should've, could've, or would've resulted . . . theoretically speaking. Simply put, you use the *conditional tense* to express a conditional action. But you can also use it to make a polite request or to subtly, or not so subtly, suggest that someone perform a certain action.

In this chapter, you investigate the regular present tense conjugations of the conditional tense. You find out how to form the conditional tense and how to use it in a sentence. And, if you so choose, you get plenty of practice to hone your conditional skills.

Forming the Regular Conditional Tense, If You Really Want To

In English, the key word to forming the conditional tense is *would*. You or somebody else *would* do something *if* the conditions were right. In Spanish, you actually change the form of the verb to build the sense of *would* right into it. When conjugating Spanish verbs in the regular conditional tense, keep the following points in mind:

✔ The regular conditional tense is a combination of the imperfect and future tenses. Check out Chapters 9 and 10 to review how to form the imperfect and future tenses.

✔ The regular conditional tense requires no spelling or stem changes.

When conjugating regular **-ar, -er,** and **-ir** verbs in the conditional tense, you simply take the entire verb infinitive (don't drop anything) and then add the imperfect verb endings you use for **-er** and **-ir** verbs.

Check out the following conjugation charts for each verb type.

preparar = to prepare	
prepararía	**prepararíamos**
prepararías	**prepararíais**
prepararía	**prepararían**
Ud. **prepararía.** = You (formal) *would prepare.*	

vender = to sell	
vendería	**venderíamos**
venderías	**venderíais**
vendería	**venderían**
Vosotras **venderíais.** = You (plural, female, familiar) *would sell.*	

escribir = to write	
escribiría	**escribiríamos**
escribirías	**escribiríais**
escribiría	**escribirían**
Ella **escribiría.** = She *would write.*	

Put the following verbs into the correct conditional form based on the subject provided. I demonstrate for you here:

Uds./saltar = *saltarían*

1. ellos/amar = _____

2. Juana/comer = _____

3. mi familia/visitar = _____

4. él/estudiar = _____

5. yo/abrir = _____

6. mi amiga/caminar = _____

7. los estudiantes/mirar = _____

8. Laura/enseñar = _____

9. nosotros/trabajar = _____

10. tú/discutir = _____

Waffling with the Conditional Tense

The conditional tense is great for waffling on issues. You can state any impossible condition or set of conditions you like and then say you would've done something if only that condition or set of conditions had been in place. It works in every language — English, Spanish, Italian, you name it — and you don't even have to be a politician to use it.

You often use the conditional tense in a sentence with two verbs, in which one verb states the condition or problem and then the second verb states, in the conditional, what you'd do under that condition or if faced with that problem. For example, in the sentence, "If I had a million dollars, I'd travel around the world," the first verb states a situation or condition, and the second verb expresses what you *would* do if that situation or condition existed.

A sentence with an *if clause* in it requires the subjunctive mood (See Chapter 12). None of the practice activities in this section uses any if clauses.

Say whether you'd do any of the following if you had a million dollars by answering *Sí* or *No*. Here's an example:

Sí ¿Investirías en el mercado de valores? *(Would you invest in the stock market?)*

11. _____ ¿Viajarías alrededor del mundo?

12. _____ ¿Comprarías una casa muy grande y ostentoso?

13. _____ ¿Compartirías el dinero con todos tus amigos y familia?

14. _____ ¿Comprarías un carro Jaguar?

15. _____ ¿Darías todo el dinero a una institución de beneficencia?

16. _____ ¿Dejarías tu trabajo?

17. _____ ¿Contratarías a una sirvienta para la casa?

18. _____ ¿Contratarías a un chófer para el carro?

19. _____ ¿Gastarías dinero desenfrenadamente?

20. _____ ¿Viajarías a Las Vegas para jugar?

Translate the following sentences into Spanish. Here's a translated question to get you started:

Would we dance all night? = *¿Bailaríamos toda la noche?*

21. Would you talk on the phone all night?

_____

22. Would she wear a dress every day?

_____

23. Would they run 100 laps?

_____

24. Would he practice the piano all day?

_____

25. Would Juan buy a new car?

_____

26. Would you open your gifts before your birthday?

_____

27. Would they open the store on Sunday?

_____

28. Could we fly to Europe?

_____

29. Could the students practice after school?

_____

30. Would the teacher listen to the students?

_____

Answer Key

Put the following verbs into the correct conditional form based on the subject provided.

1. ellos/amar = *amarían*

2. Juana/comer = *comería*

3. mi familia/visitar = *visitaría*

4. él/estudiar = *estudiaría*

5. yo/abrir = *abriría*

6. mi amiga/caminar = *caminaría*

7. los estudiantes/mirar = *mirarían*

8. Laura/enseñar = *enseñaría*

9. nosotros/trabajar = *trabajaríamos*

10. tú/discutir = *discutirías*

Say whether you'd do any of the following if you had a million dollars. Answer *Sí* or *No*. Only you know the answers here, but I provide translations of the original sentences.

11. *Sí/No* ¿Viajarías alrededor del mundo? *(Would you travel around the world?)*

12. *Sí/No* ¿Comprarías una casa muy grande y ostentoso? *(Would you buy a very large and ostentatious house?)*

13. *Sí/No* ¿Compartirías el dinero con todos tus amigos y familia? *(Would you share the money with all of your friends and family?)*

14. *Sí/No* ¿Comprarías un carro Jaguar? *(Would you buy a Jaguar car?)*

15. *Sí/No* ¿Darías todo el dinero a una institución de beneficencia? *(Would you give all of the money to a charity organization?)*

16. *Sí/No* ¿Dejarías tu trabajo? *(Would you quit your job?)*

17. *Sí/No* ¿Contratarías a una sirvienta para la casa? *(Would you hire a maid for your house?)*

18. *Sí/No* ¿Contratarías a un chófer para el carro? *(Would you hire a chauffeur for your car?)*

19. *Sí/No* ¿Gastarías dinero desenfrenadamente? *(Would you spend money in a wild shopping spree?)*

20. *Sí/No* ¿Viajarías a Las Vegas para jugar? *(Would you travel to Las Vegas to gamble?)*

Translate the following sentences into Spanish.

21. Would you talk on the phone all night?

    ¿Hablarías por teléfono toda la noche?

22. Would she wear a dress every day?

¿Llevaría ella un vestido todos los días?

23. Would they run 100 laps?

¿Correrían ellos cien vueltas?

24. Would he practice the piano all day?

¿Practicaría él el piano todo el día?

25. Would Juan buy a new car?

¿Compraría Juan un carro nuevo?

26. Would you open your gifts before your birthday?

¿Abrirías tus regalos antes de tu cumpleaños?

27. Would they open the store on Sunday?

¿Abrirían ellos la tienda el domingo?

28. Could we fly to Europe?

¿Volaríamos a Europa?

29. Could the students practice after school?

¿Practicarían los estudiantes después de la escuela?

30. Would the teacher listen to the students?

¿Escucharía el profesor a los estudiantes?

Chapter 12

Getting Wishy-Washy with the Subjunctive Mood

In This Chapter

▶ Transforming verbs into the regular present subjunctive

▶ Injecting a little doubt with the subjunctive

▶ Expressing impersonal opinions or unfinished actions

▶ More uses for the subjunctive

The subjunctive mood is tentative and uncertain. It enables you to wish, desire, and sup-pose, whenever reality falls short of expectations. It allows you to put all your short-comings behind you and suppose, just for the time being, that you're something you're not or that certain conditions are in place that aren't really in place — "If only I were rich . . ." The subjunctive mood also enables you to add a pinch of doubt to statements and offer impersonal opinions, so you can express yourself without being overly committal. It's an empowering grammatical construction.

In this chapter, you explore how to form the regular present tense subjunctive conjugations for **-ar, -er,** and **-ir** verbs, and you discover the various uses of the subjunctive, so you know when to use it and to what effect. After you find out how to form the subjunctive and when and why to use it, you're well-equipped for putting it to work in your own conversations and written communications.

The subjunctive in Spanish is called a *mood* or a *mode* rather than a *tense*, because it indi-cates the way in which the action or state of being is conceived or the attitude that the speaker has toward what she's saying.

Making the Present Subjunctive Work for You

The first step in using the subjunctive is investigating how to conjugate it. Although the method is straightforward, it varies depending on whether you're conjugating **-ar** or **-er** and **-ir** verbs. Following are the differences:

✔ For **-ar** verbs, start with the **yo** form, drop the **-o,** and add the regular endings for present-tense **-er** verbs. (Use the third-person singular ending for **yo.**)

✔ For **-er** and **-ir** verbs, start with the **yo** form, drop the **-o,** and add the regular **-ar** present-tense endings. (Again, use the third-person singular ending for **yo.**)

You can start with the verb's root and add the endings, but then you have to deal with sev-eral exceptions. By starting with the **yo** form and dropping the **-o,** you have fewer exceptions.

Regular -ar present-tense subjunctive endings:

yo -e	nosotros/as -emos
tú -es	vosotros/as -éis
él, ella -e Ud.	ellos/as -en Uds.

The verb **hablar** is always ready and willing to lend itself as an example, so I've included it here. Put **hablar** in the **yo** form, **hablo,** and then drop the **-o** and add the endings as specified. Here's what you get:

hablar = to speak	
hable	hablemos
hables	habléis
hable	hablen
Ellos **hablen.** = They *may speak*.	

Because the subjunctive mood expresses doubt, desire, uncertainty, and opinion, *may* is the best translation for the model verbs, but keep in mind that the word *may* may not always apply.

Regular -er and -ir present-tense subjunctive endings:

yo -a	nosotros/as -amos
tú -as	vosotros/as -áis
él, ella -a Ud.	ellos/as -an Uds.

Using **comer** as the model **-er** verb, start with the **yo** form, and then drop the **-o** and add the regular **-ar** present-tense endings. Here's what you get:

comer = to eat	
coma	comamos
comas	comáis
coma	coman
Yo **coma.** = I *may eat*.	

The **-ir** verbs follow the same routine. Using **vivir** as the model **-ir** verb, start with the **yo** form, and then drop the **-o** and add the regular **-ar** present-tense endings. Here's what you get:

vivir = to live	
viva	vivamos
vivas	viváis
viva	vivan
Ud. **viva.** = You (formal) *may live*.	

Staying on top of spelling changes

Several of the spelling changes come into play with the present-tense subjunctive conjugations. Note the following spelling changes:

- ✔ *z* to *c* in front of *e:*

    empezar (to begin) becomes **yo empiece** (that I may begin)

- ✔ hard *c* to *qu* in front of *e:*

    buscar (to look for) becomes **yo busque** (that I may look for)

- ✔ hard *g* to *gu* in front of *e:*

    llegar (to arrive) becomes **yo llegue** (that I may arrive)

- ✔ *gu* to *g* in front of *a:*

    seguir (to follow) becomes **yo siga** (that I may follow)

- ✔ soft *g* to *j* in front of *a:*

    proteger (to protect) becomes **yo proteja** (that I may protect)

Keeping up on stem changes

Stem-changing verbs in the subjunctive don't change stems in the **nosotros** or **vosotros** conjugations (which is the same as in the present tense), except in the following instances:

- ✔ **In -ir verbs with the stem change of *o* to *ue*, the *o* changes to *u*.**

    dormir (to sleep) becomes

    nosotros durmamos (that we may sleep)

    vosotros durmáis (that you may sleep)

- ✔ **In -ir verbs with the stem change of *e* to *ie*, the *e* changes to *i*.**

    mentir (to lie) becomes

    nosotros mintamos (that we may lie)

    vosotros mintáis (that you may lie)

- ✔ **In -ir verbs with the stem change of *e* to *i*, the *e* changes to *i*.**

    pedir (to ask for) becomes

    nosotros pidamos (that we may become)

    vosotros pidáis (that you may become)

Put the following verbs into their correct present tense subjunctive forms based on the subjects given. Here's what I mean:

Uds./pasar = *pasen*

1. nosotros/abrir = _____

2. tú/cerrar = _____

3. Pedro/hablar = _____

4. el profesor/enseñar = _____

5. el Sr. Rodríguez/vender = _____

6. Jorge/aprender = _____

7. ellos/vivir = _____

8. mis amigos/comprender = _____

9. ella/trabajar = _____

10. yo/preparar = _____

Expressing Your Innermost (and Not-So-Innermost) Desires

One of the coolest features of the subjunctive mood is that it enables you to express desire, hope, or preference; offer suggestions, recommendations, or advice; and even insist or beg for what you want. In other words, even though you may not get what you want, you can certainly ask for it, hope for it, and even insist on it. These expressions of desire, hope, and preference require a combination of two clauses:

- ✔ The main clause expresses the desire, doubt, or opinion in the indicative mood (statement of fact): for example, "I hope . . . ," "Sally advises . . . ," or "Pedro prefers . . ."

- ✔ The subordinate clause describes that which is being desired, doubted, or offered as an opinion, and you express it in the subjunctive mood. Using the first main clause (from the previous bullet) as an example: "I hope *that my package arrives tomorrow.*"

This section introduces you to the most common expressions of desire used in main clauses that require the subjunctive in the subordinate clauses. These expressions of desire are verbs that relay hope, preference, or even a recommendation.

The verbs in Table 12-1 express what the subject wants or would like to happen, but the outcome is uncertain, so the subjunctive subordinate clause is required. Stem changes are in parentheses.

Table 12-1	Verbs That Express Desire
Verb	*Translation*
aconsejar	to advise
esperar	to hope
insistir en	to insist on
mandar	to order
pedir (*e* to *i*)	to ask for, to request
preferir (*e* to *ie*)	to prefer

Verb	Translation
querer	to want
recomendar	to recommend
rogar (*o* to *ue*)	to pray, to beg
sugerir (*e* to *ie*)	to suggest

When the verb in the main clause expresses desire, the verb in the subordinate clause must be in the subjunctive. The conjunction **que** (that) connects the two clauses, and the subordinate clause (the one that requires the subjunctive) expresses uncertainty as to whether the action in the action actually occurs.

In the following examples, the conjunction is <u>underlined</u>, and the subordinate clause is in *italics*:

✔ **Él <u>recomienda</u> que *yo llegue temprano*.** = He recommends that I arrive early.

✔ **Ellos <u>prefieren</u> que *nosotros no paguemos*.** = They prefer that we not pay.

Translate the following sentences into Spanish. Here's an example:

The counselor advises that the students study abroad for one year.

La consejera aconseja que los estudiantes estudien un año en el extranjero.

11. I hope that they arrive in time.

_____

12. She prefers that the students don't talk during the exam.

_____

13. My mother insists that we eat pizza every Friday.

_____

14. They suggest that you not eat before going to bed.

_____

15. The teacher advises that the students walk slowly in the hallway.

_____

16. He orders (commands) that they open their books to page 100.

_____

17. My parents suggest that I sleep eight hours every night.

_____

18. They prefer that we clean our rooms every week.

_____

19. You (familiar) recommend that he order (request) the house specialty (*la especialidad de la casa*).

_____

20. I pray that they receive their wishes.

_____

Conveying Doubt, Impersonal Opinion, or Incomplete Action

The subjunctive mood typically is positive, enabling subjects to hope, prefer, and insist, but it doesn't need to be positive. It simply needs to be uncertain, and uncertainty can take many forms, including:

- **Doubt:** For the optimist, the subjunctive offers hope. For the pessimist, the subjunctive offers doubt. The subject doubts or can't imagine that something or other happens.

- **Impersonal opinion:** When you want to put forth an opinion without taking credit or blame for it, you can use the subjunctive to express impersonal opinion. In English, the key word in expressing impersonal opinion is *it's*. For example, "It's important that . . . ," "It's necessary that . . . ," or "It's preferable that . . ."

- **Incomplete action:** Some connecting words and phrases, such as *unless, before,* and *in case,* introduce subordinate clauses that express incomplete action. In such cases, the subjunctive mood expresses uncertainty, because the action has not yet been completed.

Voicing your doubts and reservations

Like English, Spanish uses several words to express doubt, including, of course, the verb *doubt* itself. Each verb that expresses some form of doubt must be followed by the subjunctive in order to convey the sense of uncertainty. The list in Table 12-2 contains common verbs that express doubt in Spanish.

Table 12-2	Verbs That Express Doubt
Verb	*Translation*
dudar	to doubt
no creer	to not believe
no estar convencido/a de	to not be convinced
no estar seguro/a de	to not be sure
no imaginarse	to not imagine

Verb	Translation
no parecer	to not seem
no pensar	to not think
no suponer	to not suppose
temer	to suspect, to fear

You could put together a sentence like this one to show that you're uncertain:

Yo dudo que ella llegue a tiempo. = I doubt that she arrives on time.

Although the verbs listed in the negative use the subjunctive in their subordinate clauses, these same verbs require the indicative when used in the affirmative.

Expressing impersonal opinion

When you want to express an opinion but don't necessarily want that opinion attributed to you, you can use the subjunctive to express impersonal opinion. The list of commonly used Spanish expressions in Table 12-3 state an impersonal opinion and require the subjunctive in the subordinate clause.

These expressions convey impersonal opinion by expressing emotion, uncertainty, unreality, or an indirect or implied command.

Table 12-3	Common Expressions of Impersonal Opinion
Term	*Translation*
es fantástico	it's fantastic
es importante	it's important
es imposible	it's impossible
es increíble	it's incredible
es (una) lástima	it's a shame
es mejor	it's better
es necesario	it's necessary
es posible	it's possible
es probable	it's probable
es preferible	it's preferable
es ridículo	it's ridiculous
es terrible	it's terrible
ojalá	I hope, God willing
puede ser	it may be

Here's a sentence that expresses impersonal opionion:

Es necesario que ellos trabajen más. = It's necessary that they work more.

Making one action conditional upon another

When one action is conditional upon another uncertain action, you use the subjunctive to convey that uncertainty. In the sentence, "I'll clean their room as soon as they leave," for example, the main clause, "I'll clean their room," is conditional upon the subordinate clause, "as soon as they leave." Several connecting phrases cue the use of the subjunctive, including the following terms in Table 12-4.

Table 12-4	Connecting Phrases That Use the Subjunctive
Term	*Translation*
a menos que	unless
antes (de) que*	before
con tal (de) que*	provided that
cuando	when
después (de) que*	after
en caso de que	in case
hasta que	until
mientras que	while
para que	so that, in order that
tan pronto como	as soon as

* The **de** may be omitted.

When the subordinate clause describes uncertain, incomplete action, the verb in the main clause usually is in the future tense. (For more information about the future tense, see Chapter 10.)

Here's a sentence that uses the future tense and the subjunctive mood:

Yo le hablaré tan pronto como llegue. = I'll speak will him as soon as he arrives.

Translate the following sentences into Spanish. I have included examples of doubt, impersonal opinion, and incomplete action in this activity. Check out my sample translation first:

I will wait at the train station until they arrive.

Yo esperaré en la estación de tren hasta que ellos lleguen.

21. The teacher doubts that the students study enough.

_____

22. It's possible that he is at home.

_____

23. I won't prepare the dinner unless they call.

_____

24. The students will study more so that they will pass the exam.

_____

25. It's necessary that they win the game.

_____

26. It's a shame that she doesn't cook.

_____

27. It's terrible that they never call.

_____

28. It's incredible that he works 12 hours every day.

_____

29. They'll sing until the teacher orders them to stop.

_____

30. He'll begin the concert as soon as they all arrive.

_____

31. They won't return until the game is over.

_____

32. It is necessary that you clean your room every week.

_____

33. It is important that the students attend the school every day.

_____

34. It is ridiculous that he earns so much money.

_____

35. I doubt that she prepares the dinner on time.

_____

Wrapping Up the Uses of the Subjunctive

The subjunctive is incredibly versatile, and you use it for even more than expressing doubt, voicing an impersonal opinion, or setting up a conditional action. In this section, I introduce you to further situations that call for the subjunctive. You can use the subjunctive mood

✔ In an adjectival clause if the antecedent is someone or something that is indefinite, negative, vague, or nonexistent. For example:

> **Ellos buscan un cocinero quien** = They are looking for a cook who
> **prepare comida china**   prepares Chinese food.

> **No hay nadie aquí quien corra** = There is no one here who runs faster than her.
> **más rapido que ella.**

> **¿Hay alguién en tu escuela** = Does anyone at your school speak Russian?
> **que hable ruso?**

✔ After the adverbs **acaso, quizás,** and **tal vez,** which all mean _perhaps_. For example:

> **Quizás ellos lleguen mañana.** = Perhaps they will arrive tomorrow.

✔ After **aunque** (_although_ or _even if_) if the action has not yet occurred. For example:

> **Aunque no gane, lo intentará.** = Although he may not win, he will try.

Translate the following sentences into Spanish. Here's an example:

Perhaps he studies more. = _Quizás él estudie más._

36. Even if he yells at them, they won't stop running.

_____

37. Although they may arrive tonight, I'm not waiting.

_____

38. Maybe she always studies with him.

_____

39. Perhaps the dog eats vegetables.

_____

40. Maybe they live near the ocean.

_____

41. We're looking for a chauffeur who speaks French and Spanish.

_____

42. I need a cook who can prepare three meals every day.

_____

43. There is no one at the school who speaks Spanish.

_____

44. We are looking for an apartment that doesn't cost too much.

_____

45. Even if he gets everything on the list, he will still cry.

_____

Answer Key

Put the following verbs into their correct present tense subjunctive forms based on the subjects given.

1. nosotros/abrir = *abramos*

2. tú/cerrar = *cierres*

3. Pedro/hablar = *hable*

4. el profesor/enseñar = *enseñe*

5. el Sr. Rodríguez/vender = *venda*

6. Jorge/aprender = *aprenda*

7. ellos/vivir = *vivan*

8. mis amigos/comprender = *comprendan*

9. ella/trabajar = *trabaje*

10. yo/preparar = *prepare*

Translate the following sentences into Spanish.

11. I hope that they arrive in time.

    Yo espero que ellos lleguen a tiempo.

12. She prefers that the students don't talk during the exam.

    Ella prefiere que los estudiantes no hablen durante el examen.

13. My mother insists that we eat pizza every Friday.

    Mi madre insiste en que nosotros comamos pizza todos los viernes.

14. They suggest that you not eat before going to bed.

    Ellos sugieren que tú no comas antes de acostarte.

15. The teacher advises that the students walk slowly in the hallway.

    El profesor aconseja que los estudiantes caminen despacio en el corredor.

16. He orders (commands) that they open their books to page 100.

    Él manda que ellos abran sus libros a la página cien.

17. My parents suggest that I sleep eight hours every night.

    Mis padres sugieren que yo duerma ocho horas cada noche.

18. They prefer that we clean our rooms every week.

    Ellos prefieren que nosotros limpiemos nuestros cuartos cada semana.

19. You (familiar) recommend that he order (requests) the house specialty _(la especialidad de la casa)_.

    Tú recomiendas que él pida la especialidad de la casa.

20. I pray that they receive their wishes.

    Yo ruego que ellos reciban sus deseos.

Translate the following sentences into Spanish. I have included examples of doubt, impersonal opinion, and uncompleted action in this activity.

21. The teacher doubts that the students study enough.

    El profesor duda que los estudiantes estudien bastante.

22. It's possible that he is at home.

    Es posible que él esté en casa.

23. I won't prepare the dinner unless they call.

    Yo no prepararé la cena a menos que ellos llamen.

24. The students will study more so that they will pass the exam.

    Los estudiantes estudiarán más para que aprueben el examen.

25. It's necessary that they win the game.

    Es necesario que ellos ganen el partido.

26. It's a shame that she doesn't cook.

    Es una lástima que ella no cocine.

27. It's terrible that they never call.

    Es terrible que ellos nunca llamen.

28. It's incredible that he works 12 hours every day.

    Es increíble que él trabaje doce horas cada día.

29. They'll sing until the teacher orders them to stop.

    Ellos cantarán hasta que el profesor les mande parar.

30. He'll begin the concert as soon as they all arrive.

    Él empezará el concierto tan pronto como ellos lleguen.

31. They won't return until the game is over.

    Ellos no regresarán hasta que el partido termine.

32. It is necessary that you clean your room every week.

    Es necesario que tú limpie tu cuarto cada semana.

33. It is important that the students attend the school every day.

    Es importante que los estudiantes asistan a la escuela todos los días.

34. It is ridiculous that he earns so much money.

    Es ridículo que él gane tanto dinero.

35. I doubt that she prepares the dinner on time.

    Yo dudo que ella prepare la cena a tiempo.

    Translate the following sentences into Spanish.

36. Even if he yells at them, they won't stop running.

    Aunque él los grite, no pararán de correr.

37. Although they may arrive tonight, I'm not waiting.

    Aunque ellos lleguen esta noche, yo no esperaré.

38. Maybe she always studies with him.

    Quizás ella siempre estudie con él.

39. Perhaps the dog eats vegetables.

    Quizás el perro coma verduras.

40. Maybe they live near the ocean.

    Quizás ellos vivan cerca del mar.

41. We're looking for a chauffeur who speaks French and Spanish.

    Nosotros buscamos un chófer quien hable francés y español.

42. I need a cook who can prepare three meals every day.

    Yo necesito un cocinero quien pueda preparar tres comidas cada día.

43. There is no one at the school who speaks Spanish.

    No hay nadie en la escuela quien hable español.

44. We are looking for an apartment that doesn't cost too much.

    Nosotros buscamos un apartamento que no cueste demasiado.

45. Even if he gets everything on the list, he will still cry.

    Aunque él reciba todo lo que hay en la lista, él llorará.

Chapter 13

Conveying Uncertainty about the Past with the Imperfect Subjunctive

. . . .

In This Chapter

▶ Wishing in the past tense

▶ Doubting and offering opinions about the past

▶ Expressing mannerly requests with **querer** and **poder**

▶ Presuming in the past with *if* clauses

▶ Making suppositions with *as if* or *as though*

. . . .

Hindsight isn't always 20/20. Sometimes it's more like 50/50. You may *believe* that something happened or *hope* it happened rather than *knowing* it happened. In Spanish, you use the imperfect subjunctive to express uncertainty about the past. The good news is that unlike the indicative past tense, which gives you the choice between the preterit and the imperfect (Chapter 9), the subjunctive uses only the imperfect. Whenever the verb in the main clause is in the past tense (whether preterit, imperfect, or past perfect), the subordinate clause uses the imperfect subjunctive (Chapter 13).

In this chapter, you investigate how to form the imperfect subjunctive and then use it in various statements to express wishes, doubt, or opinions about the past.

The indicative mood states facts. The subjunctive mood expresses subjective observations, wishes, desires, doubts, preferences, opinions, and anything else that is not an objective fact.

Forming the Imperfect Subjunctive

Every tense and mood has its own quirky formation that you must follow to conjugate the verb. In the case of the imperfect subjunctive, here's what you do:

1. **Start with the third-person plural form of the preterite (Chapter 9).**

2. **Drop the -ron ending to establish the verb's base.**

    This verb base is used for all verbs whether they're regular, irregular, stem-changing, or spelling-change verbs.

3. **Add the common endings from the list that follows:**

yo -ra	nosotros/as -ramos
tú -ras	vosotros/as -rais
él, ella -ra Ud.	ellos/as -ran Uds.

You can use the following endings, instead:

yo -se	nosotros/as -semos
tú -ses	vosotros/as -seis
él, ella -se Ud.	ellos/as -sen Uds.

The following tables respectively show an example of an **-ar, -er,** and **-ir** regular verb conjugated into the imperfect subjunctive.

hablar = to speak	
hablara	**habláramos**
hablaras	**hablarais**
hablara	**hablaran**
Mi padre prohibió que yo **hablara** por teléfono después de las 11:00 de la noche. = My father prohibited that I *talk* on the phone after 11:00 p.m.	

comer = to eat	
comiera	**comiéramos**
comieras	**comierais**
comiera	**comieran**
Mi padre dudaba que nosotros **comiéramos** toda la pizza. = My father doubted that we *ate* the whole pizza.	

abrir = to open	
abriera	**abriéramos**
abrieras	**abrierais**
abriera	**abrieran**
Ellos deseaban que su padre **abriera** la puerta. = They wished that his father *would open* the door.	

The vowel that precedes the **nosotros** ending is always accented.

Put the following verbs in the correct imperfect subjunctive form based on the subject provided, as I show you in the following example:

Uds./preguntar = *preguntaran*

1. él/terminar = _____

2. nosotros/cantar = _____

3. ellos/buscar = _____

4. yo/asistir a = _____

5. mi madre/pedir = _____

6. los estudiantes/abrir = _____

7. Elena/perder = _____

8. ella/encontrar = _____

9. tú/dormir = _____

10. mis amigos/salir = _____

Wishing, Doubting, and Opining About the Past

Whenever you express uncertainty about a past action, you use the imperfect subjunctive, but several key words and circumstances can also clue you in to the need for the imperfect subjunctive, like the following:

- ✔ Verbs, such as **desear** (to wish), **prohibir** (to forbid), and **creer** (to believe), when used to introduce a subordinate clause concerning an uncertain event that occurred in the past

- ✔ Expressions of personal opinion about past events that are introduced with **que** (that)

- ✔ The conjunctions **a fin de que** (in order that or so that) and **sin que** (without)

Introducing uncertainty with uncertain verbs

Some verbs naturally call for the use of the subjunctive; some of these verbs are listed in Chapter 12. Table 13-1 shows a list of additional verbs that, when followed by **que**, always require the subjunctive in the **que** clause:

Table 13-1	Verb Expressions That Require the Subjunctive
Term	**Translation**
alegrarse de que	to be happy about something
creer que (only in the affirmative)	to believe
desear que	to wish
impedir que	to prevent
negar que	to deny
pensar que (only in the affirmative)	to think
permitir que	to allow
prohibir que	to forbid
sentir que	to feel
suplicar que	to beg

Chapter 12 covers the present subjunctive. This chapter focuses on the imperfect subjunctive.

Translate the following sentences into Spanish, as in the example that follows:

He wishes that they gave more money.

Él desea que ellos dieran más dinero.

11. I believe that they arrived late last night.

   _____

12. He is happy that she finished her composition on time.

   _____

13. They think that he ran last week.

   _____

14. She denies that they ate all of the cake.

   _____

15. He prevented them from attending classes every day. (**Hint:** He prevented that they attend the classes every day.)

   _____

16. I think that they traveled to Europe last summer.

   _____

17. He denied that they entered the school late.

   _____

18. My mother fears that they used all of the money last year.

   _____

19. They wish that the train arrived on time.

   _____

20. I believe that she studied in Spain last year.

   _____

Expressing yourself in uncertain terms

Chapter 12 includes some impersonal expressions that require the subjunctive in the dependent clause. Table 13-2 gives some additional expressions in the imperfect tense that require the imperfect subjunctive.

Table 13-2	Expressions That Require the Imperfect Subjunctive
Imperfect expression	*Translation*
Era menester que	It was necessary that
Era preciso que	It was mandatory that
Era urgente que	It was urgent that
Era natural que	It was natural that
Era justo que	It was fair that
Era interesante que	It was interesting that
Era mejor que	It was better that
Convenía que	It was suitable that
Importaba que	It was important that
Parecía mentira que	It was hard to believe that

Introducing uncertainty with uncertain conjunctions

Conjunctions smooth the transition from the main clause to the subordinate clause. When these conjunctions express uncertainty, they must be followed by the subjunctive. Following are two conjunctions that always require the use of the subjunctive.

- ✔ **a fin de que** = in order that, so that
- ✔ **sin que** = without

Using the preceding impersonal expressions and conjunctions, translate the following sentences into Spanish, as I show you here:

It was interesting that they didn't say anything about their mother.

Era interesante que ellos no dieran nada de su madre.

21. She ordered less food so that they would finish on time.

_____

22. It was necessary that they earn more money.

_____

23. It was natural that she finish first.

_____

24. It was fair that he received the prize.

_____

25. It was mandatory that they pay all the money on time.

_____

26. It was urgent that she talk to him soon.

_____

27. It was important that the students study a lot for the exam.

_____

28. It was hard to believe that you traveled around the world.

_____

29. It was suitable that she taught the class.

_____

30. It was fair that Juan returned first.

_____

Ordering and Asking Politely with the Imperfect Subjunctive

In polite society, you don't tell your host, "I want this or that." You say something like, "I would like this or that." You don't ask someone, "Can you do such and such?" Instead, you say something like "Would you please do such and such?" Proper manners also are important in Spanish. To express yourself politely in Spanish, you use the imperfect subjunctive along with one of the following two words:

✔ **Querer,** which literally means _to want._ Rather than using the verb in the straight present tense, which would translate rather brusquely to "I want," use the imperfect subjunctive, which adds a much more subtle and polite sound to the request. "Quisiera una hamburguesa," for example, translates as, "I would like a hamburger."

✔ **Poder,** which literally means _to be able to_ or _can._ Rather than use the present tense (which translates as "Can you do such and such?") or the future tense (which translates to "Will you do such and such?") use the imperfect subjunctive. "¿Si pudieras, lavarías los platos?" for example, translates very politely as, "If you could, would you wash the dishes?"

Translate these orders and requests into Spanish using the imperfect subjunctive, as I show you in the following example.

Could they drive you to the airport? = *¿Pudieran ellos manejarte al aeropuerto?*

31. I would like a new Spanish book.

_____

32. Would you finish the dinner, please?

_____

33. They would like 30 new dictionaries.

_____

34. We would like to leave on time.

_____

35. Could you set the table, please?

_____

Speaking of Possibilities with If

The word *if* is packed to the gills with uncertainty; hence, it always calls for the use of the subjunctive.

Si yo fuera más inteligente, iría = If I were smarter, I would go to
a la universidad. college.

In this example, you're starting the sentence with the subordinate clause, which requires that *were* be in the imperfect subjunctive. The main clause, *I would go to college,* is in the indicative (Chapter 12).

PRACTICE

Translate the following sentences into Spanish. Here's an example:

If I had a bigger house, I would have more parties.

Si yo tuviera una casa más grande, yo tendría más fiestas.

36. If he were faster, he would win the race.

_____

37. If we had more money, we would buy a new car.

_____

38. If they had more time, they would visit all of the museums.

_____

39. If she could remember the answer, she would tell us.

_____

40. If he weren't so lazy, he would finish the work.

_____

Supposing with As if or As though

As if . . . has achieved slang status in the English language, essentially meaning *I can't believe what you're saying.* In Spanish, the phrase hasn't quite achieved slang status, but it does imply a sense that you're assuming something is true. To say *as if* or *as though* in Spanish, you use the expression **como si.**

When a subordinate clause begins with **como si,** the verb is in the imperfect subjunctive. The main clause can either be in the present, the past, or the conditional.

Here are some examples of sentences using *as if* and/or *as though.*

> **Ella actuaba como si ganara el premio.** = She acted as though she had won the prize.
> **Él hablaba como si supiera todas** = He talked as if he knew all of the answers.
> **las respuestas.**

Translate the following sentences into Spanish, as I show you in the following example:

His friends looked as if they were surprised to see him. = *Sus amigos aparecieron como si fueran sorprendidos a verlo.*

41. They looked as if they didn't know the answer.

_____

42. We felt as if we needed more sleep.

_____

43. He talked as if he deserved all of the money.

_____

44. She sings as if she has had lessons.

_____

45. The team played as if they hadn't practiced.

_____

46. They acted as if they were happy to be together.

_____

47. The students act as if they don't want to pass the test.

_____

48. My father acted as if he were happy to see us.

_____

49. They talked as if they were good friends.

_____

50. You look as if you are happy to be here.

_____

Answer Key

Put the following verbs in the correct imperfect subjunctive form based on the subject provided.

1. él/terminar = *terminara*

2. nosotros/cantar = *cantáramos*

3. ellos/buscar = *buscaran*

4. yo/asistir a = *asistiera a*

5. mi madre/pedir = *pidiera*

6. los estudiantes/abrir = *abrieran*

7. Elena/perder = *perdiera*

8. ella/encontrar = *encontrara*

9. tú/dormir = *durmieras*

10. mis amigos/salir = *salieran*

Translate the following sentences into Spanish.

11. I believe that they arrived late last night.

    Yo creo que ellos llegaran tarde anoche.

12. He is happy that she finished her composition on time.

    Él se alegra de que ella terminara su composición a tiempo.

13. They think that he ran last week.

    Ellos piensan que él corriera la semana pasada.

14. She denies that they ate all of the cake.

    Ella niega que ellos comieran todo el pastel.

15. He prevented them from attending the classes every day. (**Hint:** He prevented that they attend the classes every day.)

    Él impidió que ellos asistieran a las clases todos los días.

16. I think that they traveled to Europe last summer.

    Yo pienso que ellos viajaran a Europa el verano pasado.

17. He denied that they entered the school late.

    Él niega que ellos entraran a la escuela tarde.

18. My mother fears that they used all of the money last year.

    Mi madre teme que ellos usaran todo el dinero el año pasado.

19. They wish that the train arrived on time.

    Ellos desean que el tren llegara a tiempo.

20. I believe that she studied in Spain last year.

    Yo creo que ella estudiara en España el año pasado.

    Using the above impersonal expressions and conjunctions, translate the following sentences into Spanish.

21. She ordered less food so that they would finish on time.

    Ella pidió menos comida a fin de que ellos terminaran a tiempo.

22. It was necessary that they earn more money.

    Era necesario que ellos ganaran más dinero.

23. It was natural that she finish first.

    Era natural que ella terminara primero.

24. It was fair that he received the prize.

    Era justo que él recibiera el premio.

25. It was mandatory that they pay all the money on time.

    Era preciso que ellos pagaran todo el dinero a tiempo.

26. It was urgent that she talk to him soon.

    Era urgente que ella le hablara pronto.

27. It was important that the students study a lot for the exam.

    Era importante que los estudiantes estudiaran mucho para el examen.

28. It was hard to believe that you traveled around the world.

    Parecía mentira que tú viajaras alrededor del mundo.

29. It was suitable that she taught the class.

    Convenía que ella enseñara la clase.

30. It was fair that Juan returned first.

    Era justo que Juan regresara primero.

Translate these orders and requests into Spanish using the imperfect subjunctive.

31. I would like a new Spanish book.

Quisiera un nuevo libro de español.

32. Would you finish the dinner, please?

¿Si pudieras, terminarías la cena, por favor?

33. They would like 30 new dictionaries.

Ellos quisieran treinta diccionarios nuevos.

34. We would like to leave on time.

Nosotros quisieramos salir a tiempo.

35. Could you set the table, please?

¿Si pudieras, pondrías la mesa, por favor?

Translate the following sentences into Spanish.

36. If he were faster, he would win the race.

Si él fuera más rápido, ganaría la carre.

37. If we had more money, we would buy a new car.

Si tuviéramos más dinero, compraríamos un carro nuevo.

38. If they had more time, they would visit all of the museums.

Si tuvieran más tiempo, visitarían todos los museos.

39. If she could remember the answer, she would tell us.

Si ella pudiera recordar la respuesta, nos diría.

40. If he weren't so lazy, he would finish the work.

Si él no fuera tan perezoso, terminaría el trabajo.

Translate the following sentences into Spanish.

41. They looked as if they didn't know the answer.

Los parecían como si no supieran la respuesta.

42. We felt as if we needed more sleep.

Nosotros nos sentíamos como si necesitáramos dormir más.

43. He talked as if he deserved all of the money.

Él hablaba como si mereciera todo el dinero.

44. She sings as if she has had lessons.

   Ella canta como si tuviera lecciones.

45. The team played as if they hadn't practiced.

   El equipo jugaba como si no hubieran practicado.

46. They acted as if they were happy to be together.

   Ellos actuaban como si fueran alegres estar juntos.

47. The students act as if they don't want to pass the test.

   Los estudiantes actuan como si no quisieran aprobar el examen.

48. My father acted as if he were happy to see us.

   Mi padre actuaba como si fuera contento vernos.

49. They talked as if they were good friends.

   Ellos hablaban como si fueran buenos amigos.

50. You look as if you are happy to be here.

   Tú pareces como si fueras alegre estar aquí.

Part IV
Coping with Irregular Verbs

The 5th Wave   By Rich Tennant

"I called ahead and told Morris I'd love to have flautas for dinner tonight, so we'll see how he did."

In this part . . .

Every crowd has a few irregulars — rule breakers who simply choose to be different. When it comes to Spanish verbs, the rule breakers are the *irregular verbs* — verbs that drastically change their stems or spellings through their conjugations. They're Spanish verb outlaws, following no predictable patterns and heeding no rules or regulations. The only way to master these rogue verbs is to study them and memorize their conjugation charts.

The chapters in this part introduce the most common irregular verbs by tense and mood, so you can quickly identify them and master their conjugation charts. Each chapter focuses on a specific tense or mood to give you a command of irregularities in the present, preterit, imperfect, future, conditional, present subjunctive, and imperfect subjunctive.

Chapter 14

Dealing with Present Irregularities

● ●

● ●

*E*ven the present tense has its irregularities — verbs that refuse to conform to the rules of proper conjugations. In Spanish, verbs that are irregular in the present tense fall into two categories:

✔ Verbs that are irregular only in the **yo** form.

✔ Verbs that are irregular in any or all forms.

Verbs that are irregular only in the **yo** pose no great challenge, because for the most part they're regular. After you learn the single irregularity, they're pretty easy to deal with. Verbs that are irregular in any and all forms pose a greater challenge, simply because they're so unpredictable. The irregularities follow no set pattern. To deal with them, you have two choices — memorize the verbs and their irregularities or keep your conjugation charts handy.

In this chapter, you encounter the most common verbs that have irregular formations in the present tense, and you find out how to deal with them.

Meeting Common Verbs with Irregular Yo Forms

Verbs with **yo** form irregularities aren't just irregular — they're pretty weird. You have verbs like **caber** (to fit), which morphs into **quepo,** and verbs like **dar** (to give), which becomes **doy.** Neither rhyme nor reason seem to govern their irregularities.

Table 14-1 lists the more commonly used irregular verbs. They are presented in their infinitive forms with their meanings and then in their **yo** forms.

Table 14-1	Common Verbs That Are Irregular in the Yo Form	
Verb Infinitive	*Translation*	*Yo Form*
caber	to fit	**quepo**
caer	to fall	**caigo**
dar	to give	**doy**
hacer	to make, to do	**hago**

(continued)

Table 14-1 (continued)

Verb Infinitive	Translation	Yo Form
poner	to put	pongo
saber	to know a fact, to know how to	sé
salir	to go out, to leave	salgo
traer	to bring	traigo
valer	to be worth	valgo
ver	to see	veo

To conjugate these verbs into any other form, you simply follow the regular conjugation rules for either an **-ar, -er,** or **-ir** verb (see Chapter 2).

Hanging Out with the Present Tense Irregulars

Most irregular verbs are consistent in their weirdness. They break the rules in all of their present-tense forms; although you'll quickly see that some of these verbs have regularly formed **nosotros/as** and **vosotros/as** forms.

Because these verbs are so irregular, the best way to deal with them is to memorize their conjugation charts (by rote), so you won't have to think twice when conjugating them.

The following charts list five of the most commonly used present-tense irregular verbs. I include each verb's meaning and conjugated forms.

decir = to tell	
digo	decimos
dices	decís
dice	dicen
Yo **digo.** = I *tell*.	

oír = to hear	
oigo	oímos
oyes	oís
oye	oyen
Ud. **oye.** = You (formal) *hear*.	

oler = to smell	
huelo	olemos
hueles	oléis
huele	huelen
Tú **huele . . .** = You (familiar) *smell . . .*	

reír = to laugh	
río	reímos
ríes	reís
ríe	rien
Yo **río.** = I *laugh.*	

tener = to have	
tengo	tenemos
tienes	tenéis
tiene	tienen
Ellas **tienen.** = They (female) *have.*	

Check out Chapter 5 for common yet irregular forms of the verbs **venir** (to come) and **ir** (to go). See Chapter 7 for practice with the verbs **ser** and **estar** (to be).

Put the following verbs into their correct present-tense conjugations according to the subjects given. Here's an example:

Pedro/oler = *huele*

1. Felipe/reír = _____

2. ellos/tener = _____

3. yo/ver = _____

4. tú/oír = _____

5. los chicos/decir = _____

6. la Sra. Gómez/tener = _____

7. yo/caer = _____

8. Uds./reír = _____

9. nosotros/oler = _____

10. yo/traer = _____

Translate the following sentences into Spanish, as I show you in the following example:

She smells onions. = *Ella huele cebollas.*

11. We have 20 new books.

_____

12. I put my computer on the desk.

_____

13. They come to class every day.

_____

14. She has a new car.

_____

15. They laugh a lot.

_____

16. My mother always tells the truth.

_____

17. He hears the other students when they sing.

_____

18. I know how to speak Spanish.

_____

19. Raquel laughs all of the time.

_____

20. I see a lot from this window.

_____

Answer Key

Put the following verbs into their correct present-tense conjugations according to the subjects given.

1. Felipe/reír = *ríe*

2. ellos/tener = *tienen*

3. yo/ver = *veo*

4. tú/oír = *oyes*

5. los chicos/decir = *dicen*

6. la Sra. Gómez/tener = *tiene*

7. yo/caer = *caigo*

8. Uds./reír = *rien*

9. nosotros/oler = *olemos*

10. yo/traer = *traigo*

Translate the following sentences into Spanish.

11. We have 20 new books.

    Nosotros tenemos veinte libros nuevos.

12. I put my computer on the desk.

    Yo pongo mi computadora en el escritorio.

13. They come to class every day.

    Ellos vienen a la clase todos los días.

14. She has a new car.

    Ella tiene un carro nuevo.

15. They laugh a lot.

    Ellos rien mucho.

16. My mother always tells the truth.

    Mi madre siempre dice la verdad.

17. He hears the other students when they sing.

    Él oye a los otros estudiantes cuando cantan.

18. I know how to speak Spanish.

Yo sé hablar español.

19. Raquel laughs all of the time.

Raquel ríe todo el tiempo.

20. I see a lot from this window.

Yo veo mucho desde esta ventana.

Chapter 15

Confronting Irregularities in the Preterit Tense

In This Chapter

▶ Recognizing spelling changes in the preterit tense

▶ Identifying and manipulating stem-changing verbs in the preterit

▶ Getting a handle on variations and eccentricities by grouping like verbs

---

Irregularities in the preterit tense can make your brain hurt. They're not all that confusing; they're simply more numerous and varied than most. To help you cope, this chapter groups like verbs to lend some order to the chaos. This grouping should help you understand and memorize the various formations so they become second nature.

To survive and succeed, you need to rely on your knowledge and understanding of the present tense and what you already know about verbs. When you put it all together, the preterit tense should form a cohesive whole. Not to worry — the excessive list of irregularities that accompanies the preterit tense is not found anywhere else! Thank goodness for small favors.

 If you're not comfortable with irregular verbs in the present tense, you may want to review Chapter 14 before tackling irregularities in the preterit tense (defined in Chapter 9).

Yo! Spelling Changes in the Preterit Yo Form

The preterit tense has several irregularities that are manifested as spelling changes or, if you prefer fancier terminology, *orthographic changes*. Chapter 8 discusses these changes in detail and provides exercises to hone your skills. You need to remain aware of such spelling changes when dealing with irregularities in the preterit tense.

Spanish verbs experience the following three orthographic changes in the preterit, and they occur only in the first person singular, or **yo** form:

✔ Verbs ending in **-gar** change the *g* to *gu* in front of an *e*.

pagar becomes **yo pagué** = I paid.

✔ Verbs ending in **-car** change the *c* to *qu* in front of an *e*.

buscar becomes **yo busqué** = I looked for.

✔ Verbs ending in **-zar** change the *z* to *c* in front of an *e*.

comenzar becomes **yo comencé** = I began.

Give the correct **yo** form preterit conjugations of the following verbs, as I show you in the following example:

chocar = *choqué*

1. tocar = _____

2. practicar = _____

3. regar = _____

4. rezar = _____

5. llegar = _____

6. organizar = _____

7. jugar = _____

8. empezar = _____

9. clasificar = _____

10. tragar = _____

Changing Stems in the Preterit

As I explain in Chapter 8, some verbs experience stem changes when you conjugate them. In the present tense, stem changes occur in all three verbs types: **-ar, -er,** and **-ir.** In the preterit, however, only **-ir** verbs experience stem changes, and they occur only in the third-person/*you* formal singular (**él, ella, Ud.**) and plural (**ellos/as, Uds.**) forms of the verbs. These two factors narrow down the changes quite a bit. The following are the three types of changes that occur in the preterit:

✔ In verbs that change *o* to *ue* in the present, the *o* changes to *u*.

✔ In verbs that change *e* to *ie* in the present, the *e* changes to *i*.

✔ In verbs that change *e* to *i* in the present, the *e* changes to *i*.

In the preterit tense, stem changes occur *only* in the third-person singular and third-person plural forms.

Table 15-1 lists some verbs that have these stem changes.

Table 15-1	Common Stem-Changing Verbs	
Spelling Change	*Infinitive*	*Translation*
o to *u*	**dormir**	to sleep
	morir	to die

Spelling Change	Infinitive	Translation
e to i	advertir	to advise, to warn
	medir	to measure
	mentir	to lie
	pedir	to request, to ask for
	preferir	to prefer
	repetir	to repeat
	seguir	to follow, to continue
	(reflexive pronoun +) sentir	to feel
	servir	to serve

Put the following verbs in the correct preterit form according to the subjects I provide. Take a look at the following example before you start:

él/servir = *él sirvió*

11. tú/mentir = _____

12. ella/morir = _____

13. Tomás/seguir = _____

14. mis amigos/advertir = _____

15. la profesora/dormir = _____

16. el chico/mentir = _____

17. el cliente/pedir = _____

18. mi padre/repetir = _____

19. nosotros/preferir = _____

20. ellos/servir = _____

Following the Crowd with a Few Representative Verbs

When you're dealing with irregular verbs, sometimes the best way to proceed is to snatch a couple representatives from the crowd, learn their irregularities, and then apply what you find out to similar verbs. This section introduces some sample irregular verbs that function as representatives for various small groups of verbs that behave in much the same way.

Tagging along with decir and traer

The two verbs **decir** (to say or to tell) and **traer** (to bring) have a small group of followers, but when you're dealing with the preterit, you take any help you can get. You can find out how to conjugate these two verbs and then apply the rules to similar verbs.

Here's how these representative verbs morph in their conjugated forms:

decir = to say, to tell	
dije	dijimos
dijiste	dijisteis
dijo	dijeron
Yo **dije.** = I *said.*	

traer = to bring	
traje	trajimos
trajiste	trajisteis
trajo	trajeron
Él **trajo.** = He *brought.*	

Following are several verbs that conjugate in the preterit like **traer:**

- ✔ **atraer** = to attract
- ✔ **distraer** = to distract
- ✔ **retraer** = to bring back
- ✔ **sustraer** = to remove

Continuing the pattern with dar and ver

The verbs **dar** (to give) and **ver** (to see) have exactly the same preterit conjugated endings and a very small group of followers. What's interesting is that the verb **ver** actually follows the regular conjugation rules for **-er** preterit verbs *except* that it omits the accent marks on the first and third person singular/*you* formal **(yo and él, ella, Ud.)** forms.

Here's what these two verbs look like in the preterit:

dar = to give	
di	dimos
diste	disteis
dio	dieron
Yo **di.** = I *gave.*	

ver = to see	
vi	vimos
viste	visteis
vio	vieron
Vosotros **visteis.** = We *saw*.	

Eleven freaky verbs that share their irregularities

Now here are some freaky verbs that look and behave more like a group! These 11 verbs *all* have irregular stems in the preterit, and they all share the same irregular preterit endings. Here are the endings that all 11 of these verbs use:

yo -e	nosotros/as -imos
tú -iste	vosotros/as -isteis
él, ella -o Ud.	ellos/as -ieron Uds.

These irregular preterit endings use no accent marks.

Table 15-2 lists the 11 verbs. Each verb is presented in its infinitive form, with the definition and then the irregular preterit stem.

Table 15-2	Verbs with Irregular Preterit Stems	
Verb	*Translation*	*Irregular Preterit Stem*
andar	to walk	anduv
caber	to fit	cup
estar	to be	estuv
hacer	to do, to make	hic
haber	auxiliary verb, to have	hub
poder	to be able to	pud
poner	to put	pus
querer	to want	quis
saber	to know	sup
tener	to have	tuv
venir	to come	vin

To further complicate the scenario, some verbs have the audacity to change their meaning slightly in the preterit, so before you get into any heavy-duty exercises, expand your awareness of these subtle shifts in meaning. Table 15-3 introduces these meaning-shifters and provides their definitions in the present and preterit tenses, so you can compare them side-by-side.

Table 15-3	Verbs that Shift Meaning in the Preterit Tense	
Verb	*Present Tense Meaning*	*Preterit Tense Meaning*
conocer	to know (a person or place)	to meet
poder	to be able (to do something)	to manage (to do something)
no poder	not to be able (to do something)	to fail (to do something)
querer	to want	to try
no querer	not to want	to refuse
saber	to know (a fact/information)	to find out (learn)
sentir	to feel	to regret, to be sorry
tener	to have	to have (at a certain time)

Translate the following sentences into Spanish. Here's an example:

The movement of the cape attracted the bull. = *El movimiento de la capa atrajo el toro.*

21. I walked to the supermarket yesterday.

_____

22. She refused to go to bed at 9 p.m.

_____

23. He gave us $20.

_____

24. I had eight classes last year.

_____

25. They found out the truth last week.

_____

26. We came to the party late.

_____

27. He brought his books to the library.

_____

28. We gave the gift to the mother.

_____

29. The students put their books in the backpacks.

_____

30. She told me the same story every day.

_____

Changing i to y in the preterit

In English, some nouns change _y_ to _i_ in the plural and add _es_. In Spanish, the verbs do the changing, and the _i_ changes to _y_. A small group of **-er** and **-ir** verbs follow this pattern. When the **-er** or **-ir** ending is preceded by _i_ in the third-person singular (**él, ella, Ud.**) and plural (**ellos/as, Uds.**) and a written accent appears over the letter _i_ in all the other forms, the ending changes to a _y_. Here's an example:

creer = to believe	
creí	creímos
creíste	creísteis
creyó	creyeron
Nosotros **creímos.** = We _believed_.	

Following are some other verbs that follow this pattern:

- (reflexive pronoun +) **caer** = to fall (down)
- **leer** = to read
- **oír** = to hear
- **poseer** = to possess
- **proveer** = to provide

This rule has a couple exceptions. The verb **traer** (to bring) and the other verbs formed with **traer** don't follow this conjugation pattern. See the earlier section "A group to follow **decir** and **traer**." Also omitted are verbs ending in **-guir**, such as the verb **seguir** (to follow), because the _u_ is not pronounced but merely serves to create a hard _g_ sound.

Constructing destructive verbs like destruir

When you feel like getting a little destructive with the verb **destruir** (to destroy) and other verbs that end in **-uir**, follow the _i_-to-_y_ rule spelled out in the previous section, but be aware of one major exception. The written accent mark over the _i_ is used only in the first-person singular (**yo**) form.

I conjugated **destruir** here, so you can see what I mean.

destruir = to destroy	
destruí	destruimos
destruiste	destruisteis
destruyó	destruyeron
Vosotros **destruisteis.** = You (plural, familiar) *destroyed.*	

Following is a list of verbs that conjugate in the preterit according to the pattern shown here with **destruir:**

- ✔ **construir** = to build, to construct
- ✔ **contribuir** = to contribute
- ✔ **fluir** = to flow
- ✔ **huir** = to flee, to run away
- ✔ **incluir** = to include
- ✔ **influir** = to influence

Sharing irregularities: The verbs ser and ir

The verbs **ser** and **ir** are a couple unique oddballs that form their own dysfunctional duet. They pretend that they're two distinct verbs, but in the preterit, they look and behave exactly the same way. Just looking at them, it's tough to tell them apart. The only way to tell the difference is to obtain the meaning from the context in which the verb is used. Just look at the following conjugation chart to see what I mean:

ser = to be	ir = to go
fui	fuimos
fuiste	fuisteis
fue	fueron
Yo **fui** su amigo. = I *was* his friend.	Yo **fui** al parquet. = I *went* to the park.

Producing the preterit with verbs ending in -ucir

Not quite as weird as the verb **ser** and **ir** are verbs that end in **-ucir,** such as the model verb I've chosen for this section **traducir** (to translate). Examine the following conjugation chart to determine how to conjugate **traducir** and verbs just like it.

traducir = to translate	
traduje	tradujimos
tradujiste	tradujisteis
trudujo	trudujeron
Ella **trudujo.** = She *translated.*	

The verb **traducir** has a small group of followers, including the following verbs:

- ✔ **conducir** = to drive, to lead
- ✔ **deducir** = to deduce
- ✔ **introducir** = to introduce
- ✔ **producir** = to produce
- ✔ **reducir** = to reduce, to cut down

Using the last four groups of irregular preterit-tense verbs, give the correct preterit forms of the following verbs according the subjects provided. Here's an example:

yo/reducir = *yo reduje*

31. tú/creer = _____

32. ellos/poseer = _____

33. nosotros/incluir = _____

34. Juana/conducir = _____

35. yo/ir = _____

36. mis padres/ser = _____

37. los niños/oír = _____

38. Pilar/leer = _____

39. Uds./reducir = _____

40. el profesor/introducir = _____

Using the same group of irregular preterit verbs, translate the following sentences into Spanish, as I do in the following example:

I went to the supermarket yesterday.

Yo fui al supermercado ayer.

41. The students read four novels in English class last year.

_____

42. The recipe provided a list of ingredients.

_____

43. We fled from the house as soon as we heard the alarm.

_____

44. The tourists went to the art museum last week.

_____

45. I translated the letter for her boyfriend.

_____

46. They drove from California to New York in three days.

_____

47. The party was a surprise.

_____

48. We contributed our used clothes to the local charity.

_____

49. They constructed a new shopping mall next to the old church.

_____

50. The store reduced its prices every year after Christmas.

_____

Answer Key

Give the correct *yo* form preterit conjugations of the following verbs.

1. tocar = *toqué*

2. practicar = *practiqué*

3. regar = *regué*

4. rezar = *recé*

5. llegar = *llegué*

6. organizar = *organicé*

7. jugar = *jugué*

8. empezar = *empecé*

9. clasificar = *clasifiqué*

10. tragar = *tragué*

Put the following verbs in the correct preterit form according to the subjects provided.

11. tú/mentir = *mentiste*

12. ella/morir = *murió*

13. Tomás/seguir = *siguió*

14. mis amigos/advertir = *advirtieron*

15. la profesora/dormir = *durmió*

16. el chico/mentir = *mintió*

17. el cliente/pedir = *pidió*

18. mi padre/repetir = *repitió*

19. nosotros/preferir – *preferimos*

20. ellos/servir = *sirvieron*

Translate the following sentences into Spanish.

21. I walked to the supermarket yesterday.

    Yo anduve al supermercado ayer.

22. She refused to go to bed at 9 p.m.

    Ella no quiso acostarse a las nueve.

23. He gave us $20.

    Él nos dio veinte dólares.

24. I had eight classes last year.

    Yo tuve ocho clases el año pasado.

25. They found out the truth last week.

    Ellos supieron la verdad la semana pasada.

26. We came to the party late.

    Nosotros vinimos tarde a la fiesta.

27. He brought his books to the library.

    Él trajo sus libros a la biblioteca.

28. We gave the gift to the mother.

    Nosotros dimos el regalo a la madre.

29. The students put their books in the backpacks.

    Los estudiantes pusieron sus libros en las mochilas.

30. She told me the same story every day.

    Ella me dijo el mismo cuento todos los días.

Using the last four groups of irregular preterit tense verbs, give the correct preterit forms of the following verbs according the subjects provided.

31. tú/creer = *creíste*

32. ellos/poseer = *poseyeron*

33. nosotros/incluir = *incluímos*

34. Juana/conducir = *condujo*

35. yo/ir = *fui*

36. mis padres/ser = *fueron*

37. los niños/oír = *oyeron*

38. Pilar/leer = *leyó*

39. Uds./reducir = *redujeron*

40. el profesor/introducir = *introdujo*

Using the same group of irregular preterit verbs, translate the following sentences into Spanish.

41. The students read four novels in English class last year.

Los estudiantes leyeron cuatro novelas en la clase de inglés el año pasado.

42. The recipe provided a list of ingredients.

La receta proveyó una lista de ingredientes.

43. We fled from the house as soon as we heard the alarm.

Nosotros huimos de la casa tan pronto como oímos la alarma.

44. The tourists went to the art museum last week.

Los turistas fueron al museo de arte la semana pasada.

45. I translated the letter for her boyfriend.

Yo traduje la carta para su novio.

46. They drove from California to New York in three days.

Ellos condujeron de California a Nueva York en tres días.

47. The party was a surprise.

La fiesta fue una sorpresa.

48. We contributed our used clothes to the local charity.

Nosotros contribuimos nuestra ropa usada a la institución de beneficencia local.

49. They constructed a new shopping mall next to the old church.

Ellos construyeron un centro comercial nuevo al lado de la iglesia vieja.

50. The store reduced its prices every year after Christmas.

La tienda redujo sus precios cada año después de la Navidad.

Chapter 16

Unveiling Irregularities in the Imperfect, Future, and Conditional Tenses

. . . .

In This Chapter

▶ Taking a trip back to the regular imperfect tense

▶ Introducing three irregular imperfect verbs

▶ Presenting the irregular future and conditional verbs

. . . .

The imperfect, future, and conditional tenses are the most regular of the bunch, so I lump them all together in this chapter and deal with them as a group. Only three verbs have irregularities in the imperfect tense, so they're a snap. The future and the conditional tenses are almost as easy to manage, because they have so much in common — they share the same irregular stems when conjugated.

For comparison purposes, this chapter begins with a review of the formation of the regular imperfect tense before unveiling some of the more irregular verb formations. Then it introduces you to a trio of verbs that have some extremely irregular formations in the imperfect tense. Finally, you get a brief primer, with exercises of course, to hone your skills with the verbs that have irregularities in the future and conditional tenses.

Revisiting the Formation of the Regular Imperfect

When it comes to conjugations, calling the imperfect tense "imperfect" is a misnomer; it's the most regular of all the tenses. Almost all Spanish verbs are formed regularly in the imperfect tense. Just remember these two simple rules:

For **-ar** verbs, drop the **-ar** ending and then add the following endings:

yo -aba	nosotros/as -ábamos
tú -abas	vosotros/as -abais
él, ella -aba Ud.	ellos/as -aban Uds.

For **-er** and **-ir** verbs, drop the **-er** or **-ir** ending and then add the following endings:

yo -ía	nosotros/as -íamos
tú -ías	vosotros/as -íais
él, ella -ía Ud.	-ellos/as -ían Ud.

Give the correct imperfect forms of the following verbs according to the subjects provided. Here's an example:

los niños/salir = *los niños salían*

1. tú/decir = _____

2. nosotros/dar = _____

3. yo/hablar = _____

4. él/presentar = _____

5. ellos/conseguir = _____

6. mi madre/gastar = _____

7. los niños/dormir = _____

8. el coro/cantar = _____

9. los soldados/vencer = _____

10. ella/vender = _____

Meeting the Tres Amigos: Three Irregular Imperfect Verbs

The following three verbs are the only verbs in the Spanish language that are formed irregularly in the imperfect tense:

- ✔ **ir** = to go
- ✔ **ser** = to be
- ✔ **ver** = to see

The conjugations of these verbs don't have anything in common with one another, but with only three verbs to remember, who's complaining? The tables that follow present the conjugations for these three verbs.

ir = to go	
iba	íbamos
ibas	íbais
iba	iban
Vosotros **íbais.** = You (plural, familiar) *used to go.*	

ser = to be	
era	éramos
eras	erais
Ud. era	eran
Tú **eras.** = You *used to be.*	

ver = to see	
veía	veíamos
veías	veíais
veía	veían
Nosotros **veíamos.** = We *used to see.*	

In all of the imperfect verb formations whether *regular* or *irregular*, the first-person **(yo)** and third-person/*you* formal **(él, ella, Ud.)** singular forms are the same.

In the imperfect, you're expressing past actions that *used to* take place in a nonspecific or ongoing past period of time.

Translate the following sentences into Spanish. Here's an example:

We used to see the geese every summer. = *Nosotros veíamos los gonsos cada verano.*

11. They always went to the supermarket on Saturday.

_____

12. He used to be a soccer player.

_____

13. I used to go to Europe every year.

_____

14. The class used to see a movie every Friday.

_____

15. Shakespeare was a great writer.

_____

16. She used to see the geese every summer in the park.

_____

17. We never went to the cinema during the week.

_____

18. My father was a lawyer.

_____

19. We used to go to Chicago every summer to visit the museums.

_____

20. I saw that movie many times.

_____

Rounding Up Three Types of Irregular Future Verbs

The Spanish language has a dozen basic verbs that have irregular stems in the future tense. A dozen verbs aren't all that much to remember, but they're easier to master if you divvy them up into three groups, which is what I do in this section. The groups are based on how the irregular stems are formed.

These verbs still use the regular future endings, which are: **-é, -ás, -á, -emos, -éis,** and **-án.**

Group 1: The verbs in this group (Table 16-1) keep their regular infinitive stem with the addition of the letter *r*.

Table 16-1	Group 1: Future Stem = Infinitive Stem + *r*	
Infinitive	*Translation*	*Irregular Future Stem*
caber	to fit	cabr
haber	(helping verb) to have	habr
poder	to be able to	podr
querer	to want	querr
saber	to know a fact; to know how	sabr

Group 2: The verbs in this group (Table 16-2) keep their regular infinitive stem, with the addition of the letters *dr*.

Table 16-2	Group 2: Future Stem = Infinitive Stem + *dr*	
Infinitive	*Translation*	*Irregular Future Stem*
poner	to put	pondr
salir	to leave	saldr
tener	to have	tendr
valer	to be worth	valdr
venire	to come	vendr

Group 3: The verbs in this group (Table 16-3) change their infinitive stems entirely.

Table 16-3	Group 3: Future Stems Differ Entirely from the Infinitive	
Infinitive	*Translation*	*Irregular Future Stem*
decir	to say, to tell	dir
hacer	to do, to make	har

The verbs in Table 16-4 are derivatives of the irregular future tense verbs in three tables earlier in this section. They share the same irregular stems as their root verbs.

Table 16-4	Irregular Future Stems	
Infinitive	*Translation*	*Irregular Future Stem*
abstenerse de + infinitive	to abstain from	(reflexive pronoun +) abstendr
atenerse a	to depend or rely on	(reflexive pronoun +) atendr
componer	to compose	compondr
contener	to contain	contendr
convenir en + infinitive	to agree to do something	convendr
detener	to detain, to stop, to arrest	detendr
deshacer	to undo, to untie (a knot)	deshar
oponer	to oppose	opondr
rehacer	to redo, to remake	rehar
sostener	to sustain, to uphold	sostendr
suponer	to suppose, to assume	supondr

Translate the following sentences into Spanish, as in the following example:

The students will come tomorrow. = *Los estudiantes vendrán mañana.*

21. He will put on his uniform for the parade.

_____

22. We will leave early tomorrow.

_____

23. They will come to our house for the reception.

_____

24. I will make the cake this weekend.

_____

25. She will put the clothes in the suitcase.

_____

26. The teacher will have enough books for all of the students.

_____

27. He will become a famous doctor.

_____

28. Everyone will obtain a degree this year.

_____

29. I will oppose excessive expenses.

_____

30. That painting will be worth a lot of money in the future.

_____

Letting the Future Be Your Guide: The Irregular Conditional

The future-tense irregulars can show you everything you need to know about forming the irregular conditional, because the two share the same stems. After you commit the 12 basic verbs and their irregular stems to memory, you simply add the regular conditional verb endings and — _voilá!_ — you have the irregular conditional.

Here are the conditional verb endings:

yo -ía	nosotros/as -íamos
tú -ías	vosotros/as -íais
él, ella -ía Ud.	ellos/as -ían Uds.

The same derivative verbs that were shown in the previous section follow this same irregular conjugation pattern. See Table 16-5:

Table 16-5	Irregular Conditional Stems	
Infinitive	_Translation_	_Irregular Conditional Stem_
caber	to fit	cabr
decir	to say, to tell	dir
haber	(helping verb) to have	habr
hacer	to do, to make	har

Infinitive	Translation	Irregular Conditional Stem
poder	to be able to	podr
poner	to put	pondr
querer	to want	querr
saber	to know a fact; to know how	sabr
tener	to have	tendr
valer	to be worth	valdr
venir	to come	vendr

Put the following verbs in the correct conditional conjugation based on the subjects provided. I get you started with an example:

ella/decir = *ella diría*

31. mi padre/tener = _____

32. ellos/poder = _____

33. tú/abstener = _____

34. nosotros/decir = _____

35. Juan/querer = _____

36. él/salir = _____

37. el cliente/venir = _____

38. yo/poner = _____

39. los estudiantes/suponer = _____

40. el compositor/componer = _____

Answer Key

Give the correct imperfect forms of the following verbs according to the subjects provided.

1. tú/decir = *decías*

2. nosotros/dar = *dábamos*

3. yo/hablar = *hablaba*

4. él/presentar = *presentaba*

5. ellos/conseguir = *conseguían*

6. mi madre/gastar = *gastaba*

7. los niños/dormir = *dormían*

8. el coro/cantar = *cantaba*

9. los soldados/vencer = *vencían*

10. ella/vender = *vendía*

Translate the following sentences into Spanish.

11. They always went to the supermarket on Saturday.

Ellos siempre iban al supermercado los sábados.

12. He used to be a soccer player.

Él era un futbolista.

13. I used to go to Europe every year.

Yo iba a europa cada año.

14. The class used to see a movie every Friday.

La clase veía una película todos los viernes.

15. Shakespeare was a great writer.

Shakespeare era un gran escritor.

16. She used to see the geese every summer in the park.

Ella veía los gansos cada verano en el parque.

17. We never went to the cinema during the week.

Nosotros nunca íbamos al cine durante la semana.

18. My father was a lawyer.

Mi padre era un abogado.

19. We used to go to Chicago every summer to visit the museums.

Nosotros íbamos a Chicago cada verano a visitar los museos.

20. I saw that movie many times.

Yo veía aquella película muchas veces.

Translate the following sentences into Spanish.

21. He will put on his uniform for the parade.

Él se pondrá su uniforme para el desfile.

22. We will leave early tomorrow.

Nosotros saldremos temprano mañana.

23. They will come to our house for the reception.

Ellos vendrán a nuestra casa para la recepción.

24. I will make the cake this weekend.

Yo haré el pastel este fin de semana.

25. She will put the clothes in the suitcase.

Ella pondrá la ropa en la maleta.

26. The teacher will have enough books for all of the students.

El profesor tendrá suficientes libros para todos los estudiantes.

27. He will become a famous doctor.

Él se pondrá un médico famoso.

28. Everyone will obtain a degree this year.

Todos obtendrán un título este año.

29. I will oppose excessive expenses.

Yo opondré gastos excesivos.

30. That painting will be worth a lot of money in the future.

Aquella pintura valdrá mucho dinero en el futuro.

Put the following verbs in the correct conditional conjugation based on the subjects provided.

31. mi padre/tener = *tendría*

32. ellos/poder = *podrían*

33. tú/abstenerse = *te abstendrías*

34. nosotros/decir = *diríamos*

35. Juan/querer = *querría*

36. él/salir = *saldría*

37. el cliente/venir = *vendría*

38. yo/poner = *pondría*

39. los estudiantes/suponer = *supondrían*

40. el compositor/componer = *compondría*

Chapter 17

Mastering Subjectivity with the Irregular Present Subjunctive

- -

In This Chapter

▶ Revisiting the present subjunctive with a few irregularities

▶ Changing a verb's spelling to maintain its pronunciation in the present subjunctive

▶ Conjugating the six verbs with irregular present subjunctive forms

- -

The subjunctive mood is the mood of uncertainty, doubt, and impersonal opinion. Adding to the uncertainty is the fact that several verbs don't follow the standard operating procedure for the subjunctive mood. Some verbs demand spelling changes or stem changes in the subjunctive mood. Others follow no pattern at all.

This chapter deals specifically with the irregular present subjunctive verbs and their conjugations. If you're looking for verbs that are better behaved in the present subjunctive, review the following:

✔ The present subjunctive in Chapter 12, including the formation of the regular, stem-changing, and spelling changing verbs.

✔ Verbs with irregular **yo** forms, such as **conocer, hacer, salir,** and **tener,** as I discuss throughout this book. All verbs are considered to be regular in the present subjunctive formation if they use their present-tense **yo** form followed by the appropriate endings, even if the **yo** form is irregular.

Grappling with Spelling Changes

Spelling changes occur in certain verb conjugations to keep the pronunciation of the conjugated verb consistent with the pronunciation of the verb in its infinitive form. (See Chapter 8.) In the present subjunctive, the following spelling changes must occur to maintain proper pronunciation:

✔ The z changes to c in front of e, as in the verb **empezar** (to begin). The present tense **yo** form is **empiezo.** The present subjunctive conjugation is presented in the table that follows:

empezar = to begin	
empiece	empecemos*
empieces	empecéis*
empiece	empiecen
La profesora duda que los estudiantes **empiecen** la tarea sin su ayuda. = The professor doubts that the students *would (might) start* the assignment without her help.	
*The stem changing -**ar** and -**er** verbs don't stem change in the **nosotros** or **vosotros** forms in the present-tense subjunctive.	

Other verbs with spelling changes like **empezar** include the following. Note that **almorzar** also has a *ue* stem change.

> **almorzar** (ue) = to eat lunch
>
> **lanzar** = to hurl
>
> **tropezar** = to stumble

✔ Hard *c* changes to *qu* in front of *e,* as in the verb **buscar** (to look for). The present-tense **yo** form is **busco.** The present subjunctive conjugation is presented in the table that follows:

buscar = to look for	
busque	busquemos
busques	busquéis
busque	busquen
No vamos a encontrar el dinero a menos que lo **busquemos** por todas partes. = We won't find the money unless we *look for* it everywhere.	

Other verbs that conjugate like **buscar** include:

> **arrancar** = to root up (out), to boot up (a computer)
>
> **sacar** = to get, to take out
>
> **secar** = to dry

✔ Hard *g* changes to *gu* in front of *e,* as in the verb **llegar** (to arrive). The present tense **yo** form is **llego.** The present subjunctive conjugation is presented in the table that follows:

llegar = to arrive	
llegue	lleguemos
llegues	lleguéis
llegue	lleguen
Quizá él no **llegue** a tiempo. = Perhaps he *won't arrive* on time.	

Other verbs that conjugate like llegar include the following. **Jugar** and **rogar** also have *ue* stem changes.

> **apagar** = to put out, to turn off
>
> **jugar** (ue) = to play (a sport or a game)
>
> **pagar** = to pay
>
> **rogar** (ue) = to pray, to beg

Give the correct present subjunctive forms of the following verbs according to the subjects provided. Remember to make the appropriate spelling changes. Here's an example:

él lanzar = *él lance*

1. nosotros/pagar = _____

2. Julio/tropezar = _____

3. los estudiantes/arrancar = _____

4. yo/lanzar = _____

5. tú/jugar = _____

6. ellos/almorzar = _____

7. mi padre/rogar = _____

8. ella/sacar = _____

9. Juan y Pablo/apagar = _____

10. mi tía/secar = _____

Digging Up the Irregular Subjunctive Verbs

The bad news is that some verbs refuse to follow the pattern that most verbs follow for the present subjunctive; they don't use the present-tense **yo** form followed by the appropriate subjunctive endings. The good news is that you have only six such verbs to deal with. The best approach is to look all six of these verbs in the eye and memorize their present subjunctive conjugations as presented right here.

dar = to give	
dé	demos
des	deis
dé	den
Aunque me **des** todo su dinero no te amaré. = Even though you *may give* me all of your money I won't love you.	

estar = to be	
esté	estemos
estés	estéis
esté	estén
Tal vez ellos **estén** enfermos. = Perhaps they *are* sick.	

haber = (helping verb) to have	
haya	hayamos
hayas	hayáis
haya	hayan
Quizá ellos no le **hayan** conocido. = Maybe they *haven't* met him.	

ir = to go	
vaya	vayamos
vayas	vayáis
vaya	vayan
Es necesario que nosotros **vayamos**. = It's necessary that we *go*.	

saber = to know (something)	
sepa	sepamos
sepas	sepáis
sepa	sepan
Es probable que la profesora **sepa** la respuesta. = It's probable that the professor *knows* the answer.	

ser = to be	
sea	seamos
seas	seáis
sea	sean
Más vale que tú **seas** sincero. = It is better that you *be* sincere.	

Give the correct present subjunctive form of the following verbs according to the subjects provided, as in the following example:

yo/ir = *yo vaya*

11. mis padres/ser = _____

12. ellos/ir = _____

13. tú/dar = _____

14. yo/haber = _____

15. el Sr. Rodríguez/estar = _____

16. nosotros/ir = _____

17. el profesor/saber = _____

18. el museo/ser = _____

19. los habitantes/estar = _____

20. el médico/dar = _____

Answer Key

Give the correct present subjunctive forms of the following verbs according to the subjects provided. Remember to make the appropriate spelling changes.

1. nosotros/pagar = *paguemos*

2. Julio/tropezar = *tropece*

3. los estudiantes/arrancar = *arranquen*

4. yo/lanzar = *lance*

5. tú/jugar = *juegues*

6. ellos/almorzar = *almuercen*

7. mi padre/rogar = *ruegue*

8. ella/sacar = *saque*

9. Juan y Pablo/apagar = *apaguen*

10. mi tía/secar = *seque*

Give the correct present subjunctive form of the following verbs according to the subjects provided.

11. mis padres/ser = *sean*

12. ellos/ir = *vayan*

13. tú/dar = *des*

14. yo/haber = *haya*

15. el Sr. Rodríguez/estar = *esté*

16. nosotros/ir = *vayamos*

17. el profesor/saber = *sepa*

18. el museo/ser = *sea*

19. los habitantes/estar = *estén*

20. el médico/dar = *dé*

Part V
Getting Help with the Helping Verb Haber

The 5th Wave   By Rich Tennant

@RICHTENNANT

"I'm so proud of Ted. He ordered our entire meal in Spanish, and everything came out perfect—from the sushi appetizers to the noodle and won ton soup with shrimp tempura."

In this part . . .

The verb **haber** is like a turbocharger for other Spanish verbs. With the addition of **haber,** a verb in the past tense can become more past, a conditional statement can be completed, and a future action can be finished. **Haber** turns *did* into *had done, would* into *would have,* and *will* into *will have.* It's a helping verb that completes an action. By adding **haber** to your toolbox, you equip yourself with a whole new set of tenses — the seven compound tenses.

The chapters in this part introduce you to the verb **haber** and show you how to use it to form the seven compound tenses.

Chapter 18

Presenting the Present Perfect

In This Chapter

▶ Brushing up on the present tense forms of the helping verb **haber**

▶ Forming the regular past participles for **-ar, -er,** and **-ir** verbs

▶ Meeting some common irregular past participles face to face

▶ Putting it all together to form the present perfect

Each simple tense has a corresponding compound tense — seven simple tenses, seven compound tenses. The compound tenses make actions *perfect* or complete. In English, for example, you eat in the present, but you *have eaten* in the present perfect. In other words, you're done eating in the present tense. Granted, the distinction between the past and the present perfect can be a little subtle in any language, but you'll get the hang of it.

Forming any compound tense in Spanish is essentially a two-step process:

1. Begin with the helping verb **haber,** which translates as *to have* in the desired tense (the present tense in this chapter).

2. Tack on the past participle of the main verb.

Voilá! You have the main verb expressed in the desired compound tense.

This chapter introduces the first of the seven compound tenses — the *present perfect.* You first investigate the present tense forms of **haber.** After that, you find out how to form the regular past participles. The chapter wraps up by introducing a few commonly used verbs that have irregular past participles.

Laying the Groundwork: Conjugating Haber

The secret to conjugating verbs in any compound tense is discovering how to conjugate the verb **haber** (to have) in the desired tense. After you check that out, you simply tack on the past participle of the main verb, and you're done. Here's the verb **haber** conjugated in the present tense:

haber = (helping verb) to have	
he	hemos
has	habéis
ha	han
Yo **he hablado.** = I *have spoken.*	

Making Past Participles Out of -ar, -er, and -ir Verbs

Every verb has a past participle that expresses a completed action, such as *taken, spoken,* and *danced.* Forming the past participle in English has probably become second nature to you. In Spanish, you simply need to observe the following two rules for forming the regular past participles of **-ar, -er,** and **-ir** verbs:

✔ For **-ar** verbs, drop the **-ar** of the infinitive form and add **-ado.**

✔ For **-er** and **-ir** verbs, drop the **-er** or **-ir** of the infinitive form and add **-ido.**

Forming and using the past participles is equivalent to using *-ed* or *-en* endings in English.

Table 18-1 shows examples of each type of verb:

Table 18-1	Regular Verbs and Their Past Participles
Infinitive	*Past Participle*
hablar (to speak)	**hablado** (spoken)
comer (to eat)	**comido** (eaten)
vivir (to live)	**vivido** (lived)

Put the following verbs into their past participle forms and then give their English language equivalents. Here's an example:

preguntar = *preguntado* = *asked*

1. comprar = _____ = _____

2. servir = _____ = _____

3. cantar = _____ = _____

4. vender = _____ = _____

5. estudiar = _____ = _____

6. exigir = _____ = _____

7. crecer = _____ = _____

8. pulir = _____ = _____

9. ordenar = _____ = _____

10. escoger = _____ = _____

Boning Up on Irregular Past Participles

If all verbs were as structured and disciplined as the regular -ar, -er, and -ir verbs, life as a student of the Spanish language would be a snap. Unfortunately, the Spanish language has a hefty collection of verbs that have irregular past participles. To keep these verbs from becoming too unwieldy, I've broken them down into the following two groups:

✔ **Group 1** consists of -er and -ir verbs in which a vowel immediately precedes the infinitive ending. These verbs form their past participles regularly, *but* you must add an accent mark over the *i* in the -ido ending. Verbs that end in -uir are not included. No accent mark is necessary when a verb such as **construir** (to construct) is put into the past participle form, **construido.** Table 18-2 includes some Group 1 verbs:

Table 18-2	Group 1 (Vowel + -er/-ir Verbs) Irregular Past Participles	
Verb	*Translation*	*Past Participle*
atraer	to attract	atraído
caer	to fall	caído
creer	to believe	creído
leer	to read	leído
oír	to hear	oído
poseer	to possess	poseído
sonreír	to smile	sonreído
traer	to bring	traído

✔ **Group 2** consists of verbs with irregular past participles that follow no particular pattern and thus must be memorized. Table 18-3 includes several common verbs whose past participles follow no rules:

Table 18-3	Group 2 (No Pattern) Irregular Past Participles	
Verb	*Translation*	*Past Participle*
abrir	to open	abierto
cubrir	to cover	cubierto
decir	to say, to tell	dicho
describir	to describe	descrito
descubrir	to discover	descubierto
devolver	to return (something)	devuelto
disolver	to dissolve	disuelto
envolver	to wrap (up)	envuelto

(continued)

Table 18-3 *(continued)*

Verb	Translation	Past Participle
escribir	to write	escrito
freír	to fry	frito
hacer	to make, to do	hecho
morir	to die	muerto
oponer	to oppose	opuesto
poner	to put	puesto
proveer	to provide	provisto
resolver	to resolve	resuelto
romper	to break	roto
ver	to see	visto
volver	to return	vuelto

Pumping Iron with the Present Perfect

Now that you know how to conjugate the verb **haber** in the present tense and form the past participle of some common verbs, you have everything you need to know to be able to form the present perfect. It's time to put it all together and flex your muscles with your new compound tense. As you flex, keep the following rules and regulations in mind:

✔ Use the present perfect to express or describe actions that have happened recently and/or actions that still hold true in the present, as in the sentences: "She has arrived," or "They have lived here for two years (and still do)."

✔ Never separate the verb **haber** and the past participle with any other words.

✔ When using an object pronoun with the present perfect, the pronoun must precede the conjugated form of the verb **haber.**

The sample sentences in the list that follows show the use of the present perfect:

Yo he terminado la carta. = I have finished the letter.

Ellos han empezado la casa nueva. = They have started the new house.

Ella ha leído aquella novela. = She has read that novel.

Write *Sí* or *No* to indicate whether you've done the following things today. Here's an example:

Sí ¿Has comido algo? = *(Have you eaten something?)*

11. _____ ¿Has leído el periódico?

12. _____ ¿Has visitado un museo?

13. _____ ¿Has hablado con un/a amigo/a por teléfono?

14. _____ ¿Has escrito una carta?

15. _____ ¿Has preparado una comida?

16. _____ ¿Has limpiado la casa?

17. _____ ¿Has visto una película?

18. _____ ¿Has trabajado?

19. _____ ¿Has roto algo?

20. _____ ¿Has lavado unos platos?

Translate the following sentences into Spanish, as in the following example:

You have talked with the doctor before. = *Tú has hablado con el médico antes.*

21. I have seen all of her movies.

_____

22. They have lived in Europe for 5 years.

_____

23. She has been my best friend for a long time.

_____

24. He has repaired 20 radios today.

_____

25. The professor has called all of the students.

_____

26. We have prepared a feast for the celebration.

_____

27. Susana has been to California four times.

_____

28. The Spanish class has visited that exhibit before.

_____

29. I have read that book ten times.

_____

30. She has called us many times.

_____

Answer Key

Put the following verbs into their past participle forms and then give their English language equivalent.

1. comprar = *comprado* = *bought*

2. servir = *servido* = *served*

3. cantar = *cantado* = *sung*

4. vender = *vendido* = *sold*

5. estudiar = *estudiado* = *studied*

6. exigir = *exigido* = *demanded*

7. crecer = *crecido* = *grown*

8. pulir = *pulido* = *polished*

9. ordenar = *ordenado* = *ordered*

10. escoger = *escogido* = *chosen*

Write *Sí* or *No* to indicate whether you've done the following things today. Only you know the answers, but I provide translations of the questions.

11. *Sí/No* ¿Has leído el periódico? *(Have you read the newspaper?)*

12. *Sí/No* ¿Has visitado un museo? *(Have you visited a museum?)*

13. *Sí/No* ¿Has hablado con un/a amigo/a por teléfono? *(Have you talked with a friend on the telephone?)*

14. *Sí/No* ¿Has escrito una carta? *(Have you written a letter?)*

15. *Sí/No* ¿Has preparado una comida? *(Have you prepared a meal?)*

16. *Sí/No* ¿Has limpiado la casa? *(Have you cleaned the house?)*

17. *Sí/No* ¿Has visto una película? *(Have you seen a movie?)*

18. *Sí/No* ¿Has trabajado? *(Have you worked?)*

19. *Sí/No* ¿Has roto algo? *(Have you broken something?)*

20. *Sí/No* ¿Has lavado unos platos? *(Have you washed some dishes?)*

Translate the following sentences into Spanish.

21. I have seen all of her movies.

   Yo he visto todas sus películas.

22. They have lived in Europe for 5 years.

     Ellos han vivido en Europa por cinco años.

23. She has been my best friend for a long time.

     Ella ha sido mi mejor amigo hace mucho tiempo.

24. He has repaired 20 radios today.

     Él ha reparado veinte radios hoy.

25. The professor has called all of the students.

     El profesor ha llamado a todos los estudiantes.

26. We have prepared a feast for the celebration.

     Nosotros hemos preparado un festín para la celebración.

27. Susana has been to California four times.

     Susana ha ido a California cuatro veces.

28. The Spanish class has visited that exhibit before.

     La clase de español ha visitado aquella exposición antes.

29. I have read that book ten times.

     Yo he leído aquel libro diez veces.

30. She has called us many times.

     Ella nos ha llamado muchas veces.

Chapter 19

Going Back in Time with the Pluperfect and the Preterit Perfect

In This Chapter

▶ Describing actions that happened *before* other past actions

▶ Conjugating **haber** in the imperfect and preterit tenses

▶ Adding a past participle to form the pluperfect and preterit perfect

▶ Distinguishing the difference between the pluperfect and the preterit perfect

Because most people generally perceive time as a linear progression from one event to the next, some past actions can be, well, more past than others. "After I had heard that grasshoppers were a delicacy in Mexico," for example, "I decided to try them." In English, the helping verb *had* is used along with the past participle of the main verb to form the *past perfect* or *pluperfect*. Spanish includes two past-perfect tenses:

✔ *Pluperfect* is commonly used in conversation. The pluperfect is formed with the imperfect tense of the verb **haber** followed by the past participle of the main verb.

✔ *Preterit perfect* is commonly used in formal writing and literature. The preterit perfect is formed with the preterit tense of the verb **haber** followed by the past participle of the main verb.

 In most cases, you're going to use the pluperfect. You can pretty much ignore the preterit perfect, unless you're reading or writing a novel in Spanish or presenting a formal paper. If you're studying Spanish primarily to converse, be sure to skip the parts on the preterit perfect.

Mastering the Bare-Bones Basics: Forming the Pluperfect Tense

To form the pluperfect tense, you start with the imperfect conjugation of the verb **haber** and then tack on the past participle of the main verb. Fortunately, **haber** follows the rules of regular **-er** verbs in the imperfect tense — dropping the infinitive verb ending and then add the endings **-ía, -ías, -ía, -íamos, -íais,** and **-ían.** Following is the conjugation chart you need to etch on your brain cells.

haber = (helping verb) to have	
había	habíamos
habías	habíais
había	habían
Él **había vivido.** = He *had lived*.	

Coming up with the right conjugation of **haber** is just the first step in forming your compound-verb conjugation. You must then add the past participle of the verb whose action is being described. See Chapter 18 for instructions on forming past participles.

Touching on the Preterit Perfect

Of the seven compound tenses, the preterit perfect is the one you're likely to use least often. It's a strictly formal tense that may come in handy for your reading or composition but won't come up in conversation.

To form the preterit perfect, you begin with the preterit tense of the verb **haber** and then add the past participle of the main verb. It just so happens that the preterit conjugations of **haber** are irregular, so you need to memorize the following conjugation chart.

haber = (helping verb) to have	
hube	hubimos
hubiste	hubisteis
hubo	hubieron
Él **hubo vivido.** = He *had lived.*	

Don't forget to add the past participle of the main verb. It must appear immediately following the verb **haber,** as I explain in Chapter 18.

Here's how the complete conjugation of the past participle of viajar looks:

haber viajado = to have traveled	
he viajado	hubimos viajado
hubiste viajado	hubisteis viajado
hubo viajado	hubieron viajado
Tú **hubiste viajado.** = You (familiar) *have traveled.*	

Being in the Right Tense at the Right Time

As you've probably noticed, the pluperfect and preterit tenses in Spanish have identical translations in English. Go figure! So what's the difference? Why would you use one rather than the other? Just as the imperfect and preterit tenses have subtle differences with regard to the past, so do the pluperfect and preterit tenses. The differences in this case center less on conceptual distinctions and more on the contexts in which they're used:

✔ **Pluperfect:** The pluperfect is conversational and is used in everyday speech to describe a past action that happened prior to another past action. The more recent past action typically signals the end of the previous past action, as in the following examples:

Nosotros habíamos terminado con la cena antes de que ellos llegaron. = We had finished dinner before they arrived.

Ella nos había llamado antes de visitar.	= She had called us before visiting.
Yo me había acostado después de mi programa favorito.	= I had gone to bed after my favorite program.

✔ **Preterit perfect:** The preterit perfect is used primarily in formal or literary Spanish. Here are some examples of the preterit perfect tense:

Una vez que hubimos visto toda la película, salimos del cine.	= Once we had seen all of the movie, we left the theater.
Tan pronto como ellos hubieron terminado el trabajo, recibieron el dinero.	= As soon as they had finished the work, they received the money.
Tú apenas hubiste llegado, cuando la fiesta empezó.	= You had hardly arrived, when the party began.

Table 19-1 lists conjunctions (and translations) that call for the use of the preterit perfect in the subordinate clause.

Table 19-1	Words and Phrases That Require the Preterit Perfect
Term	**Translation**
apenas	hardly
así que	so that
cuando	when
después de que	after
en cuanto	as soon as possible
ensiguida que	at once
tan pronto como	as soon as
una vez que	once

In everyday speech and writing, the preterit is used instead of the preterit perfect, as in the following example:

Tan pronto como ellos llegaron, comimos. = As soon as they had arrived, we ate.

Translate the following compound-verb expressions into Spanish using the preterit conjugations of **haber.**

Here's an example:

You had prepared = *Tú hubiste preparado*

1. I had seen = _____

2. Juan had gone = _____

3. They had eaten = _____

4. The students had listened = _____

5. You (familiar) had written = _____

6. My father had lost = _____

7. She had heard = _____

8. We had left = _____

9. He had talked = _____

10. The store had opened = _____

Write *Sí* or *No* depending upon whether you had done the following things before going to bed yesterday. Here's an example:

Sí ¿Habías hablado con tus padres? *(Had you talked with your parents?)*

11. _____ ¿Habías mirado la televisión?

12. _____ ¿Habías visto una película de horror?

13. _____ ¿Te habías cepillado los dientes?

14. _____ ¿Te habías duchado?

15. _____ ¿Habías corrido en el parque?

16. _____ ¿Habías hecho toda la tarea para mañana?

17. _____ ¿Habías estudiado el español?

18. _____ ¿Habías hecho algunos ejercicios?

19. _____ ¿Habías leído una parte de una novela?

20. _____ ¿Habías escogido la ropa para llevar mañana?

Translate the following sentences into Spanish using the pluperfect tense, as I show you here:

I had left the purse under the chair.

Yo había dejado la bolsa debajo de la silla.

21. She had prepared the dinner before they arrived.

_____

22. They had lived here for ten years when we came.

_____

23. He had called before the party.

_____

24. The teacher had graded all of the exams before the students arrived.

_____

25. He hadn't turned out the lights before going to bed.

_____

26. The students had practiced two hours before the soccer game.

_____

27. I had learned to read before turning 3 years old.

_____

28. They had eaten before we arrived.

_____

29. My father had gotten a job before we moved.

_____

30. We had cleaned the house before we left.

_____

Answer Key

Translate the following compound-verb expressions into Spanish using the preterit conjugations of **haber.**

1. I had seen = *yo hube visto*

2. Juan had gone = *Juan hubo ido*

3. they had eaten = *ellos hubieron comido*

4. the students had listened = *los estudiantes hubieron escuchado*

5. you (familiar) had written = *tú hubiste escrito*

6. my father had lost = *mi padre hubo perdido*

7. she had heard = *ella hubo oído*

8. we had left = *nosotros hubimos salido*

9. he had talked = *él hubo hablado*

10. the store had opened = *la tienda hubo abierto*

Write *Sí* or *No* depending upon whether you had done the following things before going to bed yesterday.

Only you know the answers, but I provide translations so you can make sure you understood the questions.

11. *Sí/No* ¿Habías mirado la televisión? *(Had you watched television?)*

12. *Sí/No* ¿Habías visto una película de horror? *(Had you seen a horror movie?)*

13. *Sí/No* ¿Te habías cepillado los dientes? *(Had you brushed your teeth?)*

14. *Sí/No* ¿Te habías duchado? *(Had you showered?)*

15. *Sí/No* ¿Habías corrido en el parque? *(Had you run in the park?)*

16. *Sí/No* ¿Habías hecho toda la tarea para mañana? *(Had you done all of the homework for tomorrow?)*

17. *Sí/No* ¿Habías estudiado el español? *(Had you studied Spanish?)*

18. *Sí/No* ¿Habías hecho algunos ejercicios? *(Had you done some exercises?)*

19. *Sí/No* ¿Habías leído una parte de una novela? *(Had you read part of a novel?)*

20. *Sí/No* ¿Habías escogido la ropa para llevar mañana? *(Had you chosen the clothes to wear tomorrow?)*

Translate the following sentences into Spanish using the pluperfect tense.

21. She had prepared the dinner before they arrived.

Ella había preparado la cena antes de que ellos llegaron.

22. They had lived here for ten years when we came.

Ellos habían vivido aquí por diez años cuando nosotros venimos.

23. He had called before the party.

Él nos había llamado antes de la fiesta.

24. The teacher had graded all of the exams before the students arrived.

El profesor había calificado todos los exámenes antes de que los estudiantes llegaron.

25. He hadn't turned out the lights before going to bed.

Él no había apagado las luces antes de acostarse.

26. The students had practiced two hours before the soccer game.

Los estudiantes habían practicado por dos horas antes del partido de fútbol.

27. I had learned to read before turning 3 years old.

Yo había aprendido a leer antes de cumplir tres años.

28. They had eaten before we arrived.

Ellos habían comido antes de que nosotros llegamos.

29. My father had gotten a job before we moved.

Mi padre había conseguido trabajo antes de que nos mudamos.

30. We had cleaned the house before we left.

Nosotros habíamos limpiado la casa antes de salir.

Chapter 20

Speaking of Lost Possibilities, the Future, and Probability

The compound tenses can be considered the *perfect tenses* in the sense that they express completed actions. But how can an action be completed if it occurs in the future tense or only if a pre-existing condition occurs? This chapter answers those questions by introducing the following two compound tenses:

✔ **Future perfect:** With the future perfect, you combine the future tense of the verb **haber** with the past participle of the main verb to express actions that *will have happened*.

✔ **Conditional perfect:** With the conditional perfect, you combine the conditional tense of the verb **haber** with the past participle of the main verb to express actions that *would have happened* if the specified condition existed.

To form any of the compound tenses, you begin with the verb **haber** in the desired tense and follow it with the past participle of the main verb. This chapter provides instructions on how to conjugate **haber** in the future and conditional tenses. Refer to Chapter 18 for instructions and exercises on forming the past participles for regular and irregular verbs.

Making the Future Perfect

The future perfect tense enables you to describe actions in the future that you are almost entirely sure will happen. Of course, you can never really be sure that a future action has been completed.

To form the future perfect, you follow the same two steps you take to form any of the compound tenses:

1. Begin with the verb **haber** in the appropriate tense (in this case, future tense).

2. Add the past participle of the main verb.

The only curve here is that the helping verb **haber** is formed irregularly in the future tense. You start with the irregular verb stem **habr** and add the regular future verb endings, as shown in the chart that follows.

Future verb endings for -ar, -er, and -ir verbs:

yo -é	nosotros/as -emos
tú -ás	vosotros/as -éis
él, ella -á Ud.	ellos/as -án Uds.

The following chart shows the conjugation for the verb **haber** in the future tense.

haber = (helping verb) to have	
habré	habremos
habrás	habréis
habrá	habrán
Nosotros **habremos vivido** aquí 10 años este diciembre. = We *will have lived* here 10 years this December.	

Here's how you use the helping verb haber and the past participle to create the future perfect tense.

haber terminado = to have finished	
habré terminado	habremos terminado
habrás terminado	habréis terminado
habrá terminado	habrán terminado
Yo **habré terminado** el proyecto antes de salir de vacación. = I *will have finished* the project before leaving for vacation.	

Translate the following compound-verb structures into Spanish. Here's an example:

she will have visited = *ella habrá visitado*

1. they will have eaten = _____

2. we will have finished = _____

3. I will have left = _____

4. she will have given = _____

5. my mother will have cooked = _____

6. he will have repaired = _____

7. the students will have read = _____

8. you (familiar) will have gone = _____

9. the friends will have talked = _____

10. the principal will have decided = _____

Making Excuses with the Conditional Perfect

The conditional perfect is a tense you can't live without. It enables you to provide excuses for actions that *would have* taken place *if* certain conditions had existed. "I would have arrived on time," for example, "if my car wasn't being repaired."

Forming the conditional perfect is similar to the process you follow for forming the future-perfect tense. You begin with the verb **haber** in the desired tense (in this case, the conditional tense) and then add the past participle of the main verb. To form both the future and conditional tenses of the verb **haber,** you begin with the irregular verb stem **habr** and then add the required verb endings. The following chart provides the verb endings for the conditional tense.

Conditional verb endings for -ar, -er, and -ir verbs:

yo –ía	nosotros/as -íamos
tú –ías	vosotros/as -íais
él, ella -ía Ud.	ellos/as -ían Uds.

The chart below shows the verb **haber** conjugated in the conditional tense.

haber = (helping verb) to have	
habría	habríamos
habrías	habríais
habría	habrían
Yo **habría terminado** la tarea pero estaba demasiado cansado. = I *would have finished* the assignment but I was too tired.	

Here's what the conditional perfect looks like with the verb **escribir** (to write):

haber escrito = to have written	
habría escrito	habríamos escrito
habrías escrito	habríais escrito
habría escrito	habrían escrito
Yo te **habría escrito** una carta pero no sabía tu dirección nueva. = I *would have written* you a letter but I didn't know your new address.	

Translate the following compound verb structures into Spanish, as I show you in the following example.

I would have said = *yo habría dicho*

11. she would have prepared = _____

12. they would have written = _____

13. my parents would have visited = _____

14. I would have known = _____

15. Victor would have believed = _____

16. we would have opposed = _____

17. the manager would have hired = _____

18. the professor would have tested = _____

19. you (formal) would have requested = _____

20. he would have walked = _____

Decisions, Decisions: Future Perfect or Conditional Perfect?

Conceptually speaking, the future and conditional perfect tenses are similar — each tense expresses completed action in a future time. The similarities end there, however, because the future tense expresses action that's almost sure to be completed in the future, whereas the conditional perfect carries a great deal of doubt concerning the outcome. The following sections provide additional guidelines to help you distinguish between these two compound tenses and choose the tense that best suits your needs.

Using the future perfect

The future perfect is packed with promise. Use it when the outcome is almost certain. This tense lets you

✔ Express what will have happened by a given time in the future; for example:

Nosotros habremos terminado para las dos.	= We will have finished by 2 p.m.
Ellos habrán llegado para este fin de semana.	= They will have arrived by this weekend.

Use **para** to introduce the time expressions in these sentences.

✔ Express probability or conjecture (when a slight doubt exists) of a recent past action; for example:

Ella lo habrá terminado.	= She's probably finished it.
Ellos habrán llegado.	= They must have (probably have) arrived.

Translate the following sentences into Spanish. Here's an example:

I will have eaten all of the cookies before the party.

Yo habré comido todas las galletas antes de la fiesta.

21. He will have arrived by tonight.

_____

22. She will have taught for 35 years at the end of this year.

_____

23. We will have talked on the phone for two hours by then.

_____

24. They will have worked here for ten years after next year.

_____

25. You (familiar) must have known the truth.

_____

26. The teacher probably graded all of the exams.

_____

27. My mother will have prepared the dinner by 6 p.m.

_____

28. The students will have sold all of the cookies by Friday.

_____

29. I will have called all of the guests by 10 a.m.

_____

30. The class will have finished five novels by the end of the semester.

_____

Using the conditional perfect

Use the conditional perfect to express an action that would have happened but didn't. Such sentences typically contain a dependent clause explaining why the action did not occur; this is your excuse clause — the one that gets you out of trouble.

When forming the dependent clause, keep the following two rules in mind:

- ✔ When this dependent clause begins with _but_, the verb in that clause is in the indicative (Chapter 12).
- ✔ When dependent clause begins with _if_, the verb in the clause is in the imperfect subjunctive (Chapter 13).

Following are a couple examples that show the conditional perfect at work in a real, live sentence, complete with a dependent clause:

Nosotros habríamos ido, pero teníamos = We would have gone, but we had to work.
que trabajar.

Él habría hablado con ella, pero no = He would have talked with her, but he didn't
entendía la situación. understand the situation.

Note: Use the indicative after _but_ in the dependent clause.

| Ellos habrían ganado más dinero, si hubieran trabajado más horas. | = | They would have earned more money if they had worked more hours. |
| Tú habrías salido más temprano, si ellos te hubieran llamado a tiempo. | = | You would have left earlier if they had called you on time. |

Note: Use the imperfect subjunctive after *if* in the dependent clause.

Translate the following sentences into Spanish, as I show you here:

His parents would have called the school if they had known the principal's name.

Sus padres hubieran llamado a la escuela si habrían concocido el nombre del director.

31. I would have written you a letter, but I didn't have anything to say.

_____

32. The students would have studied more if they'd had more time.

_____

33. My mother would have attended the concert, but she couldn't find her shoes.

_____

34. Felipe would have spent more money if he'd had it.

_____

35. She would have called us earlier, but she couldn't find our phone number.

_____

36. They would have walked to the supermarket, but they were too tired.

_____

37. He would have chosen the red car if he hadn't seen the black one.

_____

38. Our team would have won, but our two best players were sick.

_____

39. We would have met the train, but we arrived too late.

_____

40. She would have invited all of the students, but her mother said "no."

_____

Answer Key

Translate the following compound-verb structures into Spanish.

1. they will have eaten = *ellos habrán comido*

2. we will have finished = *nosotros habremos terminado*

3. I will have left = *yo habré salido*

4. she will have given = *ella habrá dado*

5. my mother will have cooked = *mi madre habrá cocinado*

6. he will have repaired = *él habrá reparado*

7. the students will have read = *los estudiantes habrán leído*

8. you (familiar) will have gone = *tú habrás ido*

9. the friends will have talked = *los amigos habrán hablado*

10. the principal will have decided = *el principal habrá decidido*

Translate the following compound-verb structures into Spanish.

11. she would have prepared = *ella habría preparado*

12. they would have written = *ellos habrían escrito*

13. my parents would have visited = *mis padres habrían visitado*

14. I would have known = *yo habría sabido*

15. Victor would have believed = *Víctor habría creído*

16. we would have opposed = *nosotros habríamos opuesto*

17. the manager would have hired = *el gerente habría contratado*

18. the professor would have tested = *el profesor habría examinado*

19. you (formal) would have requested = *Ud. habría pedido*

20. he would have walked = *él habría caminado*

Translate the following sentences into Spanish.

21. He will have arrived by tonight.

    Él habrá llegado para esta noche.

22. She will have taught for 35 years at the end of this year.

    Ella habrá enseñado por treinta y cinco años para el fin de este año.

23. We will have talked on the phone for two hours by then.

    Nosotros habremos hablado por teléfono por dos horas para entonces.

24. They will have worked here for ten years after next year.

    Ellos habrán trabajado aquí por diez años para el fin del próximo año.

25. You (familiar) must have known the truth.

    Tú habrás sabido la verdad.

26. The teacher probably graded all of the exams.

    El profesor habrá calificado todos los exámenes.

27. My mother will have prepared the dinner by 6 p.m.

    Mi madre habrá preparado la cena para las seis.

28. The students will have sold all of the cookies by Friday.

    Los estudiantes habrán vendido todas las galletas dulces para el viernes.

29. I will have called all of the guests by 10 a.m.

    Yo habré llamado a todos los huéspedes para las diez de la mañana.

30. The class will have finished five novels by the end of the semester.

    La clase habrá terminado cinco novelas para el fin del semestre.

Translate the following sentences into Spanish.

31. I would have written you a letter, but I didn't have anything to say.

    Yo te habría escrito una carta, pero no tenía nada que decir.

32. The students would have studied more if they'd had more time.

    Los estudiantes habrían estudiado más, si hubieran tenido más tiempo.

33. My mother would have attended the concert, but she couldn't find her shoes.

    Mi madre habría asistido al concierto, pero no podía encontrar sus zapatos.

34. Felipe would have spent more money if he'd had it.

    Felipe habría gastado más dinero, si lo tuviera.

35. She would have called us earlier, but she couldn't find our phone number.

    Ella nos habría llamado más temprano, pero no podía encontrar nuestro número de teléfono.

36. They would have walked to the supermarket, but they were too tired.

   Ellos habrían caminado al supermercado, pero estaban demasiado cansados.

37. He would have chosen the red car if he hadn't seen the black one.

   Él habría escogido el carro rojo, si no hubiera visto el negro.

38. Our team would have won, but our two best players were sick.

   Nuestro equipo habría ganado, pero los dos mejores jugadores estaban enfermos.

39. We would have met the train, but we arrived too late.

   Nosotros habríamos encontrado el tren, pero llegábamos demasiado tarde.

40. She would have invited all of the students, but her mother said "no."

   Ella habría invitado a todos los estudiantes, pero su madre decía que "no."

Chapter 21

Speculating with the Present Perfect Subjunctive

*T*he present perfect is perfect for describing actions that *have* happened. The subjunctive mood describes actions that *may* happen. Roll the two together and you get the present perfect subjunctive — a compound tense that describes actions that *may have* happened.

This chapter shows you how to form the present perfect subjunctive and provides plenty of exercises to help you hone your skills. You also investigate how to put the present perfect subjunctive to work in daily conversation and in writing.

Check out Chapter 12 for details about forming and using the present subjunctive.

Meeting the Present Perfect Subjunctive Face to Face

Like the other compound tenses, you form the present perfect subjunctive by taking the following two steps:

1. Begin with the verb **haber** conjugated in the appropriate tense (in this case, present subjunctive).

2. Add the past participle of the main verb. (See Chapter 18 for instructions on how to form past participles.)

The following chart shows the verb **haber** conjugated in the present perfect.

haber = (helping verb) to have	
haya	hayamos
hayas	hayáis
haya	hayan
Espero que ellos **hayan terminado** su trabajo a tiempo. = I hope that they *have finished* their work on time.	

Notice that the first-person (**yo**), and the third-person (**él, ella, Ud.**) singular forms of the verb **haber** are the same in the present subjunctive.

Translate the following compound structures into Spanish using the present perfect subjunctive, as the following example shows:

she may have bought = *ella haya comprado*

1. they may have practiced = _____

2. I may have called = _____

3. the children may have broken = _____

4. you (familiar) may have screamed = _____

5. my father may have put = _____

6. she may have fainted = _____

7. they may have left = _____

8. the teacher may have spoken = _____

9. the store may have opened = _____

10. we may have listened = _____

In this activity you need to practice a little bit of conjecture. Write *C* for *cierto* (true) and *F* for *falso* (false). Here's an example:

C Las esposas esperan que sus esposos les hayan comprado flores. *(Wives hope that their husbands may have bought them flowers.)*

11. _____ El profesor espera que los estudiantes hayan estudiado.

12. _____ El entrenador no está seguro de que su equipo haya practicado suficiente.

13. _____ Los padres sugieren que sus hijos hayan gastado todo su dinero en cosas frívolas.

14. _____ La profesora de francés prefiere que sus estudiantes no hayan estudiado para el examen.

15. _____ Él espera que sus amigos hayan llegado a tiempo.

16. _____ La madre duda que los niños hayan limpiado sus cuartos.

17. _____ El juez no está convencido de que el criminal haya dicho toda la verdad.

18. _____ Es posible que el criminal haya olvidado toda la verdad.

19. _____ Más vale que los estudiantes hayan estudiado un poco en vez de que no hayan estudiado nada.

20. _____ Es importante que tú hayas comprado todos los ingredientes necesarios adelantado cuando preparas una torta.

Mobilizing the Present Perfect Subjunctive

The subtle distinctions among different tenses can make deciding which tense to use tough for you. A case in point is the distinction between the present subjunctive and the present perfect subjunctive. The following guidelines should help you decide which tense is most appropriate:

✔ When the main clause of your sentence expresses doubt or desire in the present or present-perfect tense (when something *has happened*), use the subjunctive in the subordinate clause, as I discuss in Chapter 12.

Here's an example:

Yo no supongo que tú leas los mismos libros que yo.	= I don't suppose that you (might) read the same books as I.

✔ When the subordinate clause refers to an action that *may have* taken place, use the present perfect subjunctive in the subordinate clause, as shown in the following examples.

El profesor duda que todos los estudiantes hayan hecho la tarea.	= The teacher doubts that all of the students have done the homework.
Los padres prefieren que sus niños hayan comido comida saludable.	= Parents prefer that their children have eaten healthful food.
Es posible que nosotros hayamos llegado tarde.	= It's possible that we may have arrived late.

Translate the following sentences into Spanish, as I show in the following example:

It is important that you have paid for all of the repairs.

Es importante que tú hayas pagado por todos los arreglos.

21. The children hope that their parents have left them money for dinner.

_____

22. It's possible that we have seen this movie before.

_____

23. The teacher doesn't believe that they haven't cheated.

_____

24. I don't believe that I have read this book before.

_____

25. The boss doesn't think that he has stolen the money.

_____

26. I hope that they have taken the right flight.

_____

27. They suggest that everyone has eaten before leaving.

    _____

28. The parents aren't convinced that they have studied enough.

    _____

29. It's important that they have listened to the entire tape.

    _____

30. It is necessary that they have paid tuition before August 15.

    _____

Answer Key

Translate the following compound structures into Spanish using the present perfect subjunctive.

1. they may have practiced = *ellos hayan practicado*

2. I may have called = *yo haya llamado*

3. the children may have broken = *los niños hayan roto*

4. you (familiar) may have screamed = *tú hayas gritado*

5. my father may have put = *mi padre haya puesto*

6. she may have fainted = *ella se haya desmayado*

7. they may have left = *ellos hayan salido*

8. the teacher may have spoken = *el profesor haya hablado*

9. the store may have opened = *la tienda haya abierto*

10. we may have listened = *nosotros hayamos escuchado*

In this activity you need to practice a little bit of conjecture. Write *C* for *cierto* (true) and *F* for *falso* (false). I provide translations so you can make sure your best guess makes sense.

11. *C/F* El profesor espera que los estudiantes hayan estudiado. *(The teacher hopes that the students have studied.)*

12. *C/F* El entrenador no está seguro de que su equipo haya practicado suficiente. *(The coach isn't sure that his team has practiced enough.)*

13. *C/F* Los padres exigen que sus hijos hayan gastado todo su dinero en cosas frívolas. *(Parents suggest that their children have spent all of their money on frivolous things.)*

14. *C/F* La profesora de francés prefiere que sus estudiantes no hayan estudiado para el examen. *(The French teacher prefers that her students have not studied for the exam.)*

15. *C/F* Él espera que sus amigos hayan llegado a tiempo. *(He hopes that his friends have arrived on time.)*

16. *C/F* La madre duda que los niños hayan limpiado sus cuartos. *(The mother doubts that the children have cleaned their rooms.)*

17. *C/F* El juez no está convencido de que el criminal haya dicho toda la verdad. *(The judge isn't convinced that the criminal has told the whole truth.)*

18. *C/F* Es posible que el criminal haya olvidado toda la verdad. *(It is possible that the criminal has told the whole truth.)*

19. *C/F* Más vale que los estudiantes hayan estudiado un poco en vez de que no hayan estudiado nada. *(It is better that the students have studied a little rather than that they haven't studied at all.)*

20. *C/F* Es importante que tú hayas comprado todos los ingredientes necesarios adelantado cuando preparas una torta. *(It is important that you have bought all the necessary ingredients beforehand when you're preparing a cake.)*

Translate the following sentences into Spanish.

21. The children hope that their parents have left them money for dinner.

Los niños esperan que sus padres les hayan dejado dinero para la cena.

22. It's possible that we have seen this movie before.

Es posible que nosotros hayamos visto esta película antes.

23. The teacher doesn't believe that they haven't cheated.

El profesor no cree que ellos no hayan copiado.

24. I don't believe that I have read this book before.

Yo no creo que haya leído este libro antes.

25. The boss doesn't think that he has stolen the money.

El jefe no piensa que él haya robado el dinero.

26. I hope that they have taken the right flight.

Yo espero que ellos hayan despegado en el vuelo correcto.

27. They suggest that everyone has eaten before leaving.

Ellos sugieren que todos hayan comido antes de salir.

28. The parents aren't convinced that they have studied enough.

Los padres no están convencidos de que ellos hayan estudiado suficiente.

29. It's important that they have listened to the entire tape.

Es importante que ellos hayan escuchado toda la grabación.

30. It is necessary that they have paid tuition before August 15.

Es necesario que ellos hayan pagado la matrícula antes del quince de agosto.

Chapter 22

Expressing Doubts about the Past with the Pluperfect Subjunctive

Have you ever hoped or expected that something *had* happened? If so, you probably hoped or expected in the pluperfect subjunctive and probably didn't even realize you were doing it. In English, you don't really use the pluperfect subjunctive, but you use something similar to it in sentences like this one:

> I wished that I had slept before the party.

The main clause *I wished* is in the past tense, and what I wished for — *that I had slept before the party* — is in the pluperfect, which also is called the past perfect tense. And because what *I* wished for didn't happen, it's subjunctive.

Before you get into the various uses of the pluperfect subjunctive, however, you need to find out how to form it. That's the subject of the following section.

Getting Your Feet Wet with the Pluperfect Subjunctive

Like other compound tenses, you form the pluperfect subjunctive by taking the following two steps:

1. Begin with the verb **haber** conjugated in the appropriate tense (in this case, imperfect subjunctive).

2. Add the past participle of the main verb. (See Chapter 18 for instructions on how to form past participles.)

The chart that follows shows the verb **haber** conjugated in the imperfect tense.

As I explain in Chapter 13, the imperfect subjunctive has two possible sets of endings. The following chart shows the most commonly used endings. The rule for conjugating a verb into its imperfect subjunctive form is to take the third person plural form of the verb, drop the **-ron,** and add the following endings:

yo -ra	nosotros/as -ramos
tú -ras	vosotros/as -rais
él, ella -ra Ud.	ellos/as -ran Uds.

Following this rule, the conjugation of the verb **haber** into the imperfect subjunctive is shown in the following chart.

haber = (helping verb) to have	
hubiera	hubiéramos
hubieras	hubierais
hubiera	hubieran
Yo deseaba que **hubiera dormido** antes de la fiesta. = I wished that I *had slept* before the party.	

Notice that the first person singular **(yo)** and the third person singular **(él, ella, Ud.)** forms of this conjugation are the same, the same as in the present perfect subjunctive.

haber comido = to have eaten	
hubiera comido	hubieramos comido
hubieras comido	hubierais comido
hubiera comido	hubieran comido
Ellos creían que nosotros **hubieramos comido** antes de llegar. = They believed (thought) that we *had eaten* before arriving.	

Translate the following compound-verb structures into the Spanish pluperfect subjunctive. Here's an example:

she had written = *ella hubiera escrito*

1. we had gone = _____

2. I had judged = _____

3. they had written = _____

4. the class had read = _____

5. my mother had called = _____

6. the players had lost = _____

7. the chauffeur had signaled = _____

8. the store had opened = _____

9. he had promised = _____

10. you (familiar) had traveled = _____

Diving in with the Pluperfect Subjunctive

The pluperfect subjunctive expresses the same time frame as the pluperfect; that is, it expresses a past action that is more past than another past action. The difference is that the pluperfect subjunctive is used in sentences with a main clause that requires the use of the subjunctive mood in the subordinate clause.

The following sentences reveal the difference between the pluperfect indicative and the pluperfect subjunctive:

✔ **Pluperfect Indicative**

> **Yo creía que ellos habían llegado a tiempo.** = I believed that they had arrived on time.

> Note that this sentence is a statement of fact.

✔ **Pluperfect Subjunctive**

> **Yo dudaba que ella hubiera llamado.** = I doubted that she had called.

> Note that this sentence expresses doubt, so it uses the subjunctive.

For basic information about the subjunctive mood, check out Chapter 12.

Another subtle distinction you need to be able to make is between the present perfect subjunctive (see Chapter 21) and the pluperfect subjunctive. Both constructions begin with a main clause and call for the subjunctive in the subordinate clause. The present perfect subjunctive, however, refers to actions that *may have* happened, whereas the pluperfect subjunctive references an action in the subordinate clause that *possibly had* happened.

The following sentences help distinguish between present perfect and the pluperfect subjunctives:

✔ **Present Perfect Subjunctive**

> **Es importante que los estudiantes hayan leído la lección.** = It is important that the students have read the lesson.

✔ **Pluperfect Subjunctive:**

> **Yo no creía que él hubiera robado la tienda.** = I didn't believe that he had robbed the store.

Note that both of these sentences are in the subjunctive mood. Only the tense is changed.

Translate the following sentence into Spanish, as I show in the following example:

I didn't believe that she had brought enough money.

Yo no creía que ella hubiera traído suficiente dinero.

11. They hoped that the package had arrived.

_____

12. I preferred that the children had eaten before arriving.

_____

13. He insisted that they had worked in his factory for three months before receiving a raise.

   _____

   _____

14. The teacher wasn't convinced that the students had prepared sufficiently for the presentation.

   _____

   _____

15. She wasn't sure that they had bought the correct size.

   _____

16. It was impossible that they had arrived on time.

   _____

17. It was a pity that they hadn't bought a house in our neighborhood.

   _____

18. It was possible that she had seen the robbery.

   _____

19. It was incredible that they had won the championship.

   _____

20. It didn't seem that we had walked five miles.

   _____

Translate the following sentences into Spanish. Some of the sentences require the subjunctive in the subordinate clause, and some require the indicative, so be careful. Here's an example:

It was possible that they had read the instructions.

Era posible que ellos hubieran leído las instrucciones.

21. I believed everything that she had told me.

   _____

22. They were sure that they had practiced enough to win the game.

   _____

23. He doubted that he had read the instructions correctly.

   _____

24. It was possible that she had earned more money than him.

_____

25. It was better that they had left early.

_____

26. The teacher didn't think that the students had completed the exam.

_____

27. It was better that we had paid the whole amount.

_____

28. My parents suspected that he had stolen the money.

_____

29. I thought that she had talked on the telephone for two hours.

_____

30. I wasn't sure that they had returned all of the books to the library.

_____

Answer Key

Translate the following compound-verb structures into the Spanish pluperfect subjunctive.

1. we had gone = *nosotros hubiéramos ido*

2. I had judged = *yo hubiera juzgado*

3. they had written = *ellos hubieran escrito*

4. the class had read = *la clase hubiera leído*

5. my mother had called = *mi madre hubiera llamado*

6. the players had lost = *los jugadores hubieran perdido*

7. the chauffeur had signaled = *el chofer hubiera señalado*

8. the store had opened = *la tienda hubiera abierto*

9. he had promised = *él hubiera prometido*

10. you (familiar) had traveled = *tú hubieras viajado*

Translate the following sentence into Spanish.

11. They hoped that the package had arrived.

    Ellos esperaban que el paquete hubiera llegado.

12. I preferred that the children had eaten before arriving.

    Yo prefería que los niños hubieran comido antes de llegar.

13. He insisted that they had worked in his factory for three months before receiving a raise.

    Él insistió en que ellos hubieran trabajado en su fábrica por tres meses antes de recibir un aumento de sueldo.

14. The teacher wasn't convinced that the students had prepared sufficiently for the presentation.

    El profesor no estaba convencido de que los estudiantes hubieran preparado suficientemente para la presentación.

15. She wasn't sure that they had bought the correct size.

    Ella no estaba segura de que ellos hubieran comprado el tamaño correcto.

16. It was impossible that they had arrived on time.

    Fue imposible que ellos hubieran llegado a tiempo.

17. It was a pity that they hadn't bought a house in our neighborhood.

    Fue una lástima que ellos no hubieran comprado una casa en nuestro vecindario.

18. It was possible that she had seen the robbery.

    Fue posible que ella hubiera visto el robo.

19. It was incredible that they had won the championship.

    Fue increíble que ellos hubieran ganado el campeonato.

20. It didn't seem that we had walked five miles.

    No parecía que nosotros hubiéramos caminado por cinco millas.

Translate the following sentences into Spanish. Some of the sentences require the subjunctive in the subordinate clause, and some require the indicative, so be careful.

21. I believed everything that she had told me.

    Yo creía todo lo que ella me había dicho.

22. They were sure that they had practiced enough to win the game.

    Ellos estaban seguros de que habían practicado suficientemente para ganar el partido.

23. He doubted that he had read the instructions correctly.

    Él dudaba que hubiera leído las instrucciones correctamente.

24. It was possible that she had earned more money than him.

    Fue posible que ella hubiera ganado más dinero que él.

25. It was better that they had left early.

    Más valía que ellos hubieran salido temprano.

26. The teacher didn't think that the students had completed the exam.

    El profesor no pensaba que los estudiantes hubieran completado el examen.

27. It was better that we had paid the whole amount.

    Más valía que nosotros hubiéramos pagado la suma en total.

28. My parents suspected that he had stolen the money.

    Mis padres temían que él hubiera robado el dinero.

29. I thought that she had talked on the telephone for two hours.

    Yo pensaba que ella había hablado por teléfono por dos horas.

30. I wasn't sure that they had returned all of the books to the library.

    Yo no estaba seguro de que ellos hubieran devuelto todos los libros a la biblioteca.

Part VI
The Part of Tens

The 5th Wave   By Rich Tennant

@RICHTENNANT

"I just think if we're going to be in a foreign country, we should know their units of measurement better. By the way, how's your El Grande Espresso?"

In this part . . .

This part of the book is the spot for great information that didn't necessarily fit in anywhere else and for fun stuff that you can absorb quickly and use often. In this part, I provide you with ten Spanish idioms to make you sound like a native speaker, ten verbs for Spanish holidays and other special occasions. I also answer ten of the most-asked questions about Spanish and show you how to avoid ten common pitfalls. The chapters in this part are intended to provide you with plenty of real-world examples that promise to help you communicate in Spanish on a daily basis.

Chapter 23

Ten Spanish Idioms You Can Shake a Stick At

In This Chapter

▶ Picking up some Spanish slang

▶ Understanding the literal meaning of common colloquialisms

▶ Identifying some English equivalents

*E*very language has a robust collection of *idioms* — colorful expressions that may sound a little odd to nonnative speakers. In English, for example, if someone is "pulling your leg," they're probably playing a trick on you. If you're in trouble, you may be "in the doghouse." When you don't have any money, you're "broke" or "all washed up."

The Spanish language has its own collection of idioms that are important to learn and fun to explore. Perhaps with enough practice, you can become well-versed enough in the Spanish language to concoct your own colorful expressions.

Caer mal/gordo

Literally: To fall badly/fat

Figuratively: Not suited, ill fi

No ser cosa del otro jueves.

Literally: It's not a thing from another Thursday.

Figuratively: Nothing extraordinary, nothing special

Ser uña y carne (con alguien)

Literally: To be like nail and flesh (with someone)

Figuratively: To be very close, soul mates

Ser un cero a la izquierda

Literally: To be a zero to the left

Figuratively: To be useless, worthless

A donde fueres haz los que vieres.

Literally: Wherever you may go, do as you may see.

Figuratively: When in Rome, do as the Romans.

De tal palo, tal astilla.

Literally: From such a log, such chips/splinters.

Figuratively: A chip off the old block

Te conozco bacalao, aunque vengas disfrazado.

Literally: I know you codfish, although you might come disguised.

Figuratively: I know your game; I can see your intentions.

Me pone los pelos de punta.

Literally: That makes my hair stand on end.

Figuratively: That gives me the goosebumps/the creeps.

Aquí hay gato encerrado.

Literally: Here there's a hidden/locked up cat.

Figuratively: I smell a rat.

Estás tomando mi pelo.

Literally: You're taking my hair.

Figuratively: You're pulling my leg.

Chapter 24

(More Than) Ten Verbs for Special Occasions

Special occasions, by their very nature, are action-packed events — the perfect occasions to hone your verbal skills. In this chapter, I show you ten of the most common and enjoyable verbs and tell you about the traditional celebrations during which you may want to use them.

Bailar = To Dance

Siempre **bailamos** cuando celebramos. = We always *dance* when we are celebrating.

What fun is a celebration without dancing? The Mexican Hat Dance is one of the most famous dances in the world. What better partner could you choose than a hat that never gets tired and never misses a step? For the Mexican Hat Dance, you must use a tall hat with a wide brim. You put the hat on the floor, and a man and a woman dance around it. The man tries to catch the woman by chasing her around the hat. In the end the woman picks up the hat and puts it on, which signals that now the man can catch the woman and dance with her.

Bailar is a regular -ar verb. See Chapter 2 for details about how to conjugate it.

Cantar = To Sing

Yo **canto** en el coro de la iglesia. = I *sing* in the church choir.

Christmas continues to be an extremely religious celebration in South America. Most people set up decorations with an elaborate manger, and they're sure to attend the Midnight Christmas Eve Mass. After the Mass, people fill the streets to wish friends and family goodwill and to sing carols together.

Cantar is a regular -ar verb (see Chapter 2 for more about how to conjugate it).

Cocinar = To Cook

Mi madre siempre **cocina** algo especial para mi cumpleaños.	=	My mother always *cooks* something special for my birthday.

Much special cooking is done for the different holidays celebrated in the Spanish-speaking countries. One such holiday celebrated in Spain is St. John's Day, which falls on June 24. If your name is John (or Juan in Spanish) then this day is your special day, and your family will bake you a big cake in the shape of the letter *J.*

Cocinar is a regular -ar verb (see Chapter 2 for more about how to conjugate it).

Cumplir = To Complete, To Turn (So Many Years Old)

Este añi él **va a cumplir** 10 años.	=	This year he *will complete* 10 years.

In Spanish-speaking countries, people don't ask "How old are you?" They say "How many years do you have?" or "How many years have you completed?" People wish one another a happy birthday by saying **Feliz Cumpleaños,** which literally translates as "Happy Completed Years." Strange but true.

Cumplir is a regular -ir verb (see Chapter 2 for more about how to conjugate it).

Desfilar = To Parade

Ahora ellos **desfilan** en la calle.	=	Now they *are parading* in the street.

Desfiles, or parades, are common to many holidays around the world, and the Spanish-speaking countries are no exception. As a matter of fact, given their elaborate public displays of color and merry-making, you might say that they're masters at it. One Spanish holiday that features a parade is Assumption Day or **Día de la Asunción.** This day celebrates the body of Mary rising to heaven to be united with her soul in heaven. Many statues of Mary adorned with flowers and colorful ribbons are paraded through the streets.

Desfilar is a regular -ar verb (see Chapter 2 for more about how to conjugate it).

Pedir Prestado = To Borrow

Ella siempre **pide prestado** dinero para algo.	=	She always *borrows* money for something.

April Fool's Day is celebrated in Mexico but in a slightly different way. Instead of playing little tricks, people attempt to borrow items from others. If anyone is foolish enough to lend something on this of all days, the items borrowed are not returned. Instead the borrower sends the lender a poem to say that he or she has been fooled.

Pedir prestado is an "e to i" stem-changing verb (see Chapter 8 for more about how to conjugate it).

Regalar = To Give a Gift

Mis padres me **regalaron** un carro nuevo cuando me gradué. = My parents *gave* me a new car when I graduated.

El Día de los Tres Reyes, literally "The Day of the Three Kings," also called "Epiphany," is celebrated on January 6. This day is to celebrate the coming of the Three Wise Men to Bethlehem. On this day, children leave their shoes out to be filled with goodies by the Magi. The wise man named Balthazar is the favorite of the children, because he brings them gifts and candy called **turrón.**

Regalar is a regular -ar verb (see Chapter 2 for more about how to conjugate it).

Rezar = To Pray

Nosotros **rezamos** cada día. = We *pray* every day.

Much praying is done during the season of Lent while worshippers strengthen their faith in God through repentance and meditation. The Lenten season lasts 40 days and leads to the celebration of the risen Christ at Easter. The 40 days may symbolize the 40 days that Moses spent on Mount Sinai, the 40 years that the Jewish people were wandering, the 40 days that Jesus spent in the desert, or the 40 hours that Jesus was in the tomb. A modern Lenten custom is the World Day of Prayer, which is a day when Christians all around the world pray that Christ's will be done and that His peace may come to earth.

Rezar is a regular -ar verb (see Chapter 2 for more about how to conjugate it).

Tirar Agua = To Throw Water

Ellos **tiran agua** durante el carnival en unos países de latinoamérica. = They *throw water* during "Carnival" in some countries in Latin America.

Part of Carnival in some Spanish-speaking countries is water throwing. People throw water from rooftops and balconies on innocent passers by. Young men go to the houses of their girlfriends where a battle ensues during which they try to throw each other into a fountain, bathtub (filled with water), or shower. In Catholic countries, carnivals are festive days before the serious Lenten season begins. These days come to an end with the climax on Shrove Tuesday. In the United States, we have a large Carnival celebrated in New Orleans, called Mardi Gras.

Tirar is a regular -ar verb (see Chapter 2 for more about how to conjugate it).

Visitar los Cementarios = To Visit the Cemetaries; Ir de Picnic = To Picnic

En México **visitan los cementarios** y **van de picnic** como parte de la celebración del "Día de los Muertos." = In Mexico they *visit the cemeteries* and *have picnics* as part of the celebration of the "Day of the Dead."

Another uniquely Hispanic custom is the celebration of the **Día de los Muertos** or The Day of the Dead, celebrated November 2. Also known as All Soul's Day, this holiday is the equivalent of Halloween (October 31), which is actually All Hallow's Eve or the eve of All Saint's Day on November 1. Hispanic people celebrate this day to honor loved ones who have passed away. A common practice is to take a picnic to the cemetery to visit the graves of the deceased. It is important to remember to bring all of the favorite foods of the family member who has passed on, because it is believed that on this day they are allowed to return to earth to celebrate and eat with their loved ones.

Visitar is a regular -ar verb (see Chapter 2 for more about how to conjugate it).

Ir is an irregular verb (see Chapter 5 for more about how to conjugate it).

Comer Mazapán = To Eat Marzipan

Cuando estoy en España siempre **como** mazapán. = When I am in Spain I always *eat* marzipan.

Of the variety of sweets available in Spain at Christmas time, none is molded more artistically than **mazapán** (or marzipan), which came to Spain from the Arabians, who ruled Spain for nearly eight centuries. Marzipan is a delicacy made of crushed almonds with sugar and eggs mixed in. The ancient city of Toledo in Spain is the marzipan capital.

Comer is a regular -er verb (see Chapter 2 for more about how to conjugate it).

Comer Uvas = To Eat Grapes

Cuando se celebra "El Año Nuevo" en España, es tradicional **comer** 12 uvas cuando es medíanoche. = When the New Year is celebrated in Spain, it is traditional to *eat* 12 grapes at midnight.

In all cultures, eating usually is an integral part of any holiday, but Spain has a New Year's Eve custom that involves eating, not for the taste and satisfaction, but for good luck. At the stroke of midnight, revelers are supposed to eat 12 grapes, one at each strike of the hour. Everyone pops one grape at each strike of the clock and gives New Year's wishes to friends and family. The eating of the 12 grapes is to ensure that the coming year will have 12 happy months. Of course, it's best to try to get the seedless variety!

Chapter 25

Answers to the Ten Most Common Questions about Spanish

In This Chapter

▶ Distinguishing between **ser** and **estar**

▶ Listing differences in tense, mood, and mode

▶ Recognizing a diphthong when you meet one

When you learn a first language, you don't need to conceptualize the structures or use your intellect to understand grammar and usage. All that technical stuff is internalized as you gain more and more knowledge of the language. It becomes second-nature. You develop a mental schemata for structure and grammar in your brain, as you develop from a babbling baby into an eloquent adult. Some people are extremely fortunate and are taught two, three, or even more languages from birth. When that happens, the brain makes allowances for all of the different mental schemata for each of the languages.

When you're learning a second language later in life, however, the existing schemata are so well entrenched that your brain must work overtime to make the necessary adjustments. You almost have to *unlearn* one way before you can learn the new way. Not only are there thousands of new vocabulary words to memorize, but you have to integrate the new and complex grammatical structures and configurations into your already spinning head.

In an attempt to help sort out some of the most unusual or difficult of these concepts, this chapter presents what I consider to be ten of the most common difficulties that people have when learning Spanish grammar and usage.

What's the difference between por and para?

The Spanish language includes a few utility words that change meaning depending on the context. Two such words, **por** and **para,** are easy to confuse, especially for those who are learning Spanish for the first time. The following guidelines help alleviate some of the confusion:

Por is used for the following:

   ✔ To describe a means of transportation

   por avión = by plane.

   ✔ To perform multiplication

   dos **por** tres son seis = two times three equals six

✔ To do something for someone

Lo hice **por** ella. = I did it for her.

✔ To express a length of time

Juan estuvo en francía **por** tres días. = Juan was in France for three days.

✔ As the preposition *through*

Viajamos **por** tres estados. We traveled through three states.

Para is used for the following:

✔ To express purpose as *in order to* or *for*

Ella trabaja **para** ganar dinero. = She works to earn money.

Yo trabajo **para** el Sr. Gonzalez. = I work for Mr. Gonzalez.

✔ As the preposition *to*

Ellos van **para** California. = They are going to California.

Para mi sorpresa él llegó temprano. = To my surprise, he arrived early.

✔ As the preposition *by*

Debe estar listo **para** las dos. = It should be ready by 2 p.m.

What's the difference between ser and estar?

The verbs **ser** and **estar** both mean *to be*, but *being* is a concept that varies depending on its context (check out Chapter 7 for a detailed explanation of **ser** and **estar**). Here is some additional guidance that can help you make the correct choice.

Ser is used for the following:

✔ To state one's origin, or where a person is from

Él **es** de México. = He is from Mexico.

✔ To describe the qualities of a person, place, or thing

Juan Luís **es** muy inteligente. = Juan Luís is very intelligent.

Su casa **es** muy grande.= Their house is very large.

✔ To state one's profession

Mi papá **era** abogado. = My father was a lawyer.

Estar is used for the following:

✔ To specify the location of a person, place, or thing

Yo **estoy** en la biblioteca. = I am at the library.

✔ To describe one's condition or feelings

Él **está** enfermo. = He is sick.

Ellos **están** muy contentos. = They are very happy.

✔ To state the condition of a place or a thing

La puerta **está** abierta. = The door is open.

El centro comercial **está** cerrado los fines de semana. = The mall is closed on weekends.

✔ To form the present progressive

Marisol **está** estudiando ahora. = Marisol is studying now.

✔ To form the past progressive

Ellos **estaban** saliendo cuando él llegó. = They were leaving when he arrived.

What's the difference between tener que and deber?

The difference between **tener que** and **deber** generally boils down to the difference between *being compelled to do something* and *feeling morally obligated to perform the task*. **Tener que** plus an infinitive means that someone *has to* do whatever the verb infinitive states — you only *have to* die and pay taxes. On the other hand **deber** has the implication of moral obligation, as in this is what one *should* or *ought to* do." For example:

Tú **tienes que** pagar el impuesto. = You have to pay the tax.

Tú **debes** ayudar a los que necesitan ayuda. = You should (ought to) help those in need.

What's the difference between poner and ponerse?

The verbs **poner** and **ponerse** look like identical twins and sound even more alike, but they actually are quite different. **Poner** is *to put or place something somewhere,* or *to turn something on,* such as a light or a TV. Whereas **ponerse** means *to become, to put on* (clothing), or *to set* (as in the setting sun). The following examples help illustrate the distinction between the two:

Yo **puse** el libro en el escritorio. = I put the book on the desk.

Yo **puse** la luz cuando entré en la casa. = I turned on the light when I entered the house.

Él se **puso** médico. = He became a doctor.

Los miembros del equipo se **pusieron** sus uniformes. = The team members put on their uniforms.

El sol se **pone** más temprano en el invierno. = The sun sets earlier in the winter.

What's the difference between a verb tense and a mood or mode?

The *tense* of a verb tells the time of an action or state; for example, past, present or future, as in the following examples:

Yo **estudio** mucho. = I study a lot.

Yo **estudié** ayer. = I studied yesterday.

Yo **estudiaré** mañana. = I will study tomorrow.

The *mood* or *mode* of a verb is a reflection of the subject's attitude toward what the verb expresses. The main moods in Spanish are the *imperative* (or commands), the *indicative* (statements of fact), and the *subjunctive* (basically subjective — wishes, suppositions, doubts, and so on).

What's the difference between tú and usted (Ud.)?

Both **tú** and **usted (Ud.)** are *subject pronouns* that mean *you* (singular). The difference is to whom you're speaking. The pronoun **tú** is the familiar or *informal you*, because it's used when speaking to a friend or family member. On the other hand, when you want to be more respectful or when you don't know someone well, you use **usted (Ud.)**, which is referred to as the *formal you*.

What's the difference between vosotros and ustedes (Uds.)?

The pronouns **vosotros** and **ustedes (Uds.)** follow the same usage rules as **tú** and **usted** and represent their plural equivalents. **Vosotros** is *you* (plural, familiar or informal) and is used with friends and family members, whereas **ustedes (Uds.)** is *you* (plural, formal) and is used in more formal or respectful conversation. **Vosotros** is used primarily; in Spain, and in Latin America, the **ustedes** form is often used for both the informal and formal *you*.

How do you form a negative statement?

To form a negative statement in Spanish, simply add a **no** in front of the verb and any direct, indirect, or reflexive pronouns (if there are any). The following examples show you what to do:

Él **no** tiene mi anillo.	= He doesn't have my ring.
Él **no** lo tiene.	= He doesn't have it.

How do you pluralize in Spanish?

Three very simple rules apply when you want to form the plurals of nouns and adjectives in Spanish. The following chart explains what they are:

If the word ends in . . .	add . . .
a vowel	s
a consonant	es
a z	change the z to a c, and add es

What in the world is a diphthong?

In Spanish *diphthongs* are called **diptongos** — a sequence of two vowels that glide together and count as a single sound. Look for the italics in the following examples to see **diptongos** in action:

agua (ah-gwah)   = water

caimán (ky-mahn)   = alligator

Chapter 26

Avoiding Ten Common Spanish Verbs Mix-ups

In This Chapter

▶ Getting a feel for some confusing connotative nuances

▶ Describing different types of being and knowing

▶ Unearthing the many ways to play

*1*n every language, including English, a particular action can have 20 or more words to describe it, and each word can have a slightly different meaning. You can, for example, call someone — or summon or phone or beckon or contact or subpoena or . . . you get the idea.

In your native tongue, the slight variations in meaning become second nature, but when you're learning a new language, and you're looking up meanings of words in a dictionary, the subtle nuances are easy to miss. This chapter presents the ten most commonly misused verbs in the Spanish language, explains their correct usage, and provides examples to clarify their differences.

To Ask or to Ask For

Use **preguntó** only for asking questions. As I show you in the following examples:

Yo pregunté a la profesora, "¿Cuántos años tiene usted?"	= I asked the teacher, "How old are you?"
Ella siempre pregunta muchas preguntas en la clase de química.	= She always asks a lot of questions in chemistry class.

If you're asking *for*, in the sense of ordering or requesting something, the use **pedir,** properly conjugated, of course. The following sentences show you what I mean:

Ellos pidieron unas pizzas para el almuerzo.	= They ordered (requested, asked for) some pizzas for lunch.
Él pidió las direcciones para nuestra casa nueva.	= He asked for directions to our new house.

Having More Than Someone Else or Having More Than a Specific Number

When you're saying that you have more of a specific number of something, you use "más de" plus the number of the things that you have more of, as I show you in the following examples:

Él tiene más de veinte sombreros.	= He has more than twenty hats.
Ella ganó más de cien mil dólares.	= She won more than one hundred thousand dollars.

On the other hand, when you want to say that you have more of something than someone else has or you like one thing more than another, then you use "más que," as in these examples:

Nosotros tenemos más tierra que ellos.	= We have more land than they do.
A Rafael le gustan las frutas más que las verduras.	= Rafael likes fruit more than vegetables.

Knowing Someone or Something

The verbs **conocer** and **saber** both mean "to know," but they are used differently. The verb **conocer** means to know or be familiar with a person, place or thing. The following sentences show you the correct use of **conocer**:

Yo conozco a su madre.	= I know his mother.
Ellos conocen al director de la escuela.	= They know the principal of the school.
Susana conoce San Francisco.	= Susana knows (is familiar with) San Francisco.
Mi esposo conoce muy bien la música de Bob Dylan.	= My husband knows the music of Bob Dylan very well.

The verb **saber,** on the other hand, means to know something, such as a fact, or how to do something. The following sentences show you the right way to use **saber**:

Miguel sabe que ellos son de Chile.	= Miguel knows that they are from Chile.
Mi cuñado sabe volar un avión.	= My brother-in-law knows how to fly an airplane.

Leaving Something or Just Plain Leaving

The verbs **salir** and **dejar** both mean "to leave," but you should use **salir** to express the action of leaving a place, as the following examples illustrate:

Ellos salieron del teatro temprano.	= They left the theater early.
El tren sale a las dos de la tarde.	= The train leaves at 2 p.m.

When you want to say that someone left something, use **dejar** instead, as I show you in the following examples:

El hombre dejó una propina en la mesa.	=	The man left a tip on the table.
Nosotros dejamos la maleta en casa.	=	We left the suitcase at home.

Returning Something or Just Returning

Both **regresar** and **devolver** mean "to return," but you use **regresar** to describe a situation in which a person is returning. Here are some examples:

Él siempre regresa temprano de vacación.	=	He always returns early from vacation.
Nuestros hijos regresaron tarde a casa anoche.	=	Our children returned home late last night.

Use **devolver** when someone is returning an item, as I show you in the following example:

Marcela devolvió el vestido, porque era demasiado grande.	=	Marcela returned the dress because it was too large.
Los estudiantes devolvieron los libros a la biblioteca a tiempo.	=	The students returned the books to the library on time.

Spending Money or Time

The verbs **gastar** and **sasar** both mean "to spend," but Spanish actually has two distinct words to differentiate between "spending time" and "spending money." Use **gastar** to spend money (think of spending money on gas), as in the following example:

Ella siempre gasta mucho dinero en Target.	=	She always spends a lot of money at Target.
Me gusta gastar dinero.	=	I like spending money.

If you're spending time, use **pasar** (think of passing the time), as in the following example:

Cuando nosotros vamos a Florida, siempre pasamos la mayoría del tiempo en la playa.	=	When we go to Florida, we always spend the majority of the time at the beach.
Ellos pasaron dos horas en el parque ayer.	=	They spent 2 hours in the park yesterday.

Playing a Game, an Instrument, or a Role

Spanish has three verbs that translate as "to play": **jugar, tocar,** and **desempeñar,** but their meanings are far from identical.

To say that you are playing a sport or a game, you use **jugar**, as in the following example:

Los muchachos juegan al fútbol todas las tardes.	=	The boys play soccer every afternoon.
Mi padre jugó baloncesto mucho cuando era niño.	=	My father played basketball a lot when he was a child.

To say that you are playing an instrument, use **tocar**, as the following example illustrates:

Juan toca el piano en la orquesta.	=	Juan plays the piano in the orchestra.
Mi amigo siempre toca la guitarra y canta cuando nosotros tenemos una fiesta.	=	My friend always plays the guitar and sings when we have a party.

Last but not least, if you want to say that you or someone is playing a role (as in a play), use the verb **desempeñar**. Here are some examples:

Boris Karloff desempeñó la parte de Frankenstein en la película.	=	Boris Karloff played the part of Frankenstein in the movie.
Ella desempeña la parte de la heroína en mi programa favorita.	=	She plays the part of the heroine in my favorite program.

To Wake up or to Get up

To wake up is **despertarse.** You use it like this:

Mi madre se despertó a las 8:00 de la mañana ayer.	=	My mother woke up at 8:00 a.m. yesterday.
Ellos se despertaron tarde esta mañana, y por eso llegaron tarde a la escuela.	=	They woke up late this morning, and therefore arrived late to school.

To physically, get up (out of the bed) is **levantarse.** It's appropriate in sentences like these:

A Raquel le gusta levantarse tarde si no tiene nada que hacer.	=	Raquel likes to get up late if she doesn't have anything to do.
Nosotros nos levantamos a las 11:00 de la mañana el sábado pasado.	=	We got up at 11:00 a.m. last Saturday.

So you can *wake up* at 7:00 a.m., but sooner or later you have to *get up* to actually go anywhere. Of course, if you're prone to sleepwalking, you might **levantarse** before you **despertarse.**

To Leave or to Take Leave of

Salir is to physically leave from a place. You use it like this:

Mis padres salieron para el aeropuerto a las 4:00 de la tarde hoy.	=	My parents left for the airport at 4:00 p.m. today.
Ellos salieron de la fiesta temprano.	=	They left the party early.

Despedirse, on the other hand, means to take leave of, or to say "good-bye." Here are some examples:

Él siempre se despide cuando sale.	= He always says good-bye when he leaves.
Los estudiantes se despidieron a todos.	= The students said good-bye to everyone.

It Is Sunny vs. It Is Cloudy

When describing the weather in Spanish you usually use either the verb **estar** which means "to be," as in the following example:

Mañana estará nublado.	= Tomorrow it will be cloudy.

You might also use the verb **hacer,** which means "to make," as the following example shows:

Hoy hace buen tiempo.	= Today it is nice (good) weather.

Why? Well, it comes down to the weather condition itself. Use **hacer** to describe weather that has no action taking place:

Hace (mucho) sol.	= It's (very) sunny.
Hace (mucho) calor.	= It's (very) hot.
Hace (mucho) frío.	= It's (very) cold.
Hace (muy) mal tiempo.	= It's (very) bad weather.

Use **estar** to describe weather that has an action taking place:

Está nevando.	= It's snowing.
Está lloviendo.	= It's raining.

Part VII
Appendixes

The 5th Wave   By Rich Tennant

"I know it's a popular American expression, but you just don't say 'Hasta la vista, baby' to a nun.'"

In this part . . .

*E*very chapter in this book contains exercises that prompt you to translate sentences from Spanish to English or vice versa. I intentionally use very common Spanish words in the examples, so you can focus on verb conjugations without spending too much time on vocabulary. If you're a little rusty on vocabulary or you happen to experience a brain brownout and can't remember a particular word, you should be able to find it in one of these appendixes. Here, I provide two limited glossaries of words that appear in this book — a Spanish/English glossary and an English/Spanish glossary. I also provide a list of common irregular verb forms. Think of these as crib notes for the various exercises.

Appendix A
Spanish/English Glossary

abuelos (m.) = grandparents

acercarse = to approach, to near

acostarse = to go to bed

aeropuerto (m.) = airport

ajedrez (m.) = chess

alarma (f.) = alarm

alrededor de = around

amar = to love

andar = to walk

apagar = to turn off

aprender = to learn

aprobar (un examen) = to pass (a test)

arreglar = to repair

auditorio (m.) = auditorium

aumento de sueldo (m.) = raise (of salary)

avión (m.) = plane

azul = blue

biblioteca (f.) = library

blanco = white

boda (f.) = wedding

calificar = to grade (papers, exams, and so on)

calor = hot

cansado/a = tired

carrera (f.) = race

cena (f.) = dinner

centro comercial (m.) = shopping mall

cepillarse los dientes = to brush one's teeth

cerca (de) = near (to)

cerrar = to close

chofer (m.) = chauffeur

cine (m.) = cinema

compartir = to share

computadora (f.) = computer

contratar = to hire

copiar = to cheat

crecer = to grow

cuando = when

cuarto (m.) = room

de = from

dejar (el trabajo) = to quit (work)

deprimido/a = depressed

desenfrenadamente = unrestrainedly

desfile (m.) = parade

desmayarse = to faint

despertarse = to wake up

diccionario (m.) = dictionary

difícil = difficult

dinero (m.) = money

discutir = to discuss, to debate

ducharse = to shower oneself

durante = during

ejercicios (m.) = exercises

emocionado/a = excited

encontrar = to find

enseñar = to teach

entrenador/a (m., f.) = (the) coach

equipo (m.) = team

escoger = to choose

escritor/a (m., f.) = writer

escuela (f.) = school

esperar = to hope

estado (m.) = state

este, esta = this

examinar = to test

excesivo = excessive

exigir = to demand

exposición (f.) = exhibit

fábrica (f.) = factory

festín (m.) = feast

flojo/a, perezoso/a = lazy

fresco = cool

frío = cold

fútbol (m.) = soccer

gansos (m.) = geese

gastar = to spend

gastos (m.) = expenses

gimnasio (m.) = gym

grabación (f.) = tape recording

gritar = to scream

helado (m.) = ice cream

huéspedes (m.) = guests

iglesia (f.) = church

ingrediente (m.) = ingrediente

institución de beneficencia (f.) = charity organization

inteligente = intelligent

invierno = winter

ir de compras = to go shopping

juez (m.) = judge

jugar = to gamble, to play (a game or a sport)

juntos = together

juzgar = to judge

lápices (m.) = pencils

lástima = pity

lecciones (f.) lessons

levantarse = to get up

llevar = to wear

lugar (m.) = place

maleta (f.) = suitcase

matrícula (f.) = tuition

merecer = to deserve

mesa (f.) = table

millas (f.) = miles

mochila (f.) = backpack

morado = purple

música clásica (f.) = classical music

muy = very

negro = black

oponer = to oppose

otoño = autumn

pájaros (m.) = birds

paquete (m.) = package

parque (m.) = park

partido (m.) = (sports) game

pedir = to ask for

pedir = to request

película (f.) = movie

perder = to lose

periódico (m.) = newspaper

pescar = to fish

piloto/a (m., f.) = the pilot

pintar = to paint

platos (m.) = dishes

playa (f.) = beach

poner (la mesa) = to set (the table)

primavera = spring

prometer = to promise

pulir = to polish

que = that, than

química (f.) = chemistry

receta (f.) = recipe

recordar = to remember

regalo (m.) = gift

respuesta (f.) = the answer

restaurante (m.) = restaurant

río (m.) = river

robo (m.) = robbery

rojo = red

romper = to break

rosado = pink

roto/a = broken

sala (f.) = living room

salir = to leave

señalar = to signal

sirvienta (f.) = servant

sol = sun, sunny

sorpresa (f.) = surprise

suéter (m.) = sweater

suficiente = enough

supermercado (m.) = supermarket

suprimir = to suppress, to omit

tamaño (m.) = size

teatro (m.) = theater

televisión (f.) = television

temprano = early

terminar = to finish

tiempo = time

tiempo = weather

tienda (f.) = store

título (m.) = degree

todos (los domingos) = every (Sunday)

tragar = to swallow

traje de baño (m.) = swimsuit

uniforme (m.) = uniform

vecindario (m.) = neighborhood

vender = to sell

verano = summer

verdad (f.) = truth

verde = green

viajar = to travel

volar = to fly

votar = to vote

vuelta (f.) = lap

Appendix B
English/Spanish Glossary

airport = **el aeropuerto**

alarm = **la alarma**

answer = **la respuesta**

to approach, to near = **acercarse**

around = **alrededor de**

to ask for = **pedir**

auditorium = **el auditorio**

autumn = **el otoño**

backpack = **la mochila**

beach = **la playa**

birds = **los pájaros**

black = **negro**

blue = **azul**

to break = **romper**

broken = **roto/a**

to brush one's teeth = **cepillarse los dientes**

charity organization = **la institución de beneficencia**

chauffer = **el chófer**

to cheat = **copiar**

chemistry = **la química**

chess = **el ajedrez**

to choose = **escoger**

church = **la iglesia**

cinema = **el cine**

classical music = **la música clásica**

to close = **cerrar**

coach = **el/la entrenador/a**

cold = **frío**

computer = **la computadora**

cool = **fresco**

degree = **el título**

to demand = **exigir**

depressed = **deprimido/a**

to deserve = **merecer**

dictionary = **el diccionario**

difficult = **difícil**

dinner = **la cena**

to discuss, to debate = **discutir**

dishes = **los platos**

during = **durante**

early = **temprano**

enough = **suficiente**

every (Sunday) = **todos (los domingos)**

excessive = **excesivo**

excited = **emocionado/a**

exercises = **los ejercicios**

exhibit = **exposición**

expenses = **los gastos**

factory = **la fábrica**

to faint = **desmayarse**

feast = **el festín**

to find = **encontrar**

to finish = **terminar**

to fish = **pescar**

to fly = **volar**

from = **de**

to gamble = **jugar**

game (sports) = **el partido**

geese = **los gansos**

to get up = **levantarse**

gift = **el regalo**

to go to bed = **acostarse**

to grade (papers, exams, and so on) = **calificar**

grandparents = **los abuelos**

green = **verde**

to grow = **crecer**

guests = **los huéspedes**

gym = **el gimnasio**

to hire = **contratar**

to hope = **esperar**

hot = **calor**

ice cream = **el helado**

ingredient = **el ingrediente**

intelligent = **inteligente**

judge = **el juez**

to judge = **juzgar**

lap = **la vuelta**

lazy = **flojo/a, perezoso/a**

to learn = **aprender**

to leave = **salir**

lessons = **las lecciones**

library = **la biblioteca**

living room = **la sala**

to lose = **perder**

to love = **amar**

miles = **las millas**

money = **el dinero**

movie = **la película**

near (to) = **cerca (de)**

neighborhood = **el vecindario**

newspaper = **el periódico**

to oppose = **oponer**

package = **el paquete**

to paint = **pintar**

parade = **el desfile**

park = **el parque**

to pass (a test) = **aprobar (un examen)**

pencils = **los lápices**

pilot = **el/la piloto/a**

pink = **rosado**

pity = **una lástima**

place = **el lugar**

plane = **el avión**

to polish = **pulir**

to promise = **prometer**

purple = **morado**

to quit (work) = **dejar (el trabajo)**

race = **la carrera**

raise = **el aumento de sueldo**

recipe = **la receta**

red = **rojo**

to remember = **recordar**

to repair = **arreglar**

to request = **pedir**

restaurant = **el restaurante**

river = **el río**

robbery = **el robo**

room = **el cuarto**

school = **la escuela**

to scream = **gritar**

to sell = **vender**

servant = **la sirvienta**

to set (the table) = **poner (la mesa)**

to share = **compartir**

to shop = **ir de compras**

shopping mall = **el centro comercial**

to shower oneself = **ducharse**

to signal = **señalar**

size = **el tamaño**

soccer = **el fútbol**

to spend = **gastar**

spring = **la primavera**

state = **el estado**

store = **la tienda**

suitcase = **la maleta**

summer = **el verano**

sun, sunny = **sol**

supermarket = **el supermercado**

to suppress, to omit = **suprimir**

surprise = **la sorpresa**

to swallow = **tragar**

sweater = **el suéter**

swimsuit = **el traje de baño**

table = **la mesa**

tape (recording) = **la grabación**

to teach = **enseñar**

team = **el equipo**

television = **la televisión**

to test = **examinar**

that, than = **que**

theater = **el teatro**

this = **este, esta**

time = **el tiempo, la hora**

tired = **cansado**

together = **juntos**

to travel = **viajar**

truth = **la verdad**

tuition = **la matrícula**

to turn off = **apagar**

uniform = **el uniforme**

unrestrainedly = **desenfrenadamente**

very = **muy**

to vote = **votar**

to wake up = **despertarse**

walk = **andar**

to wear = **llevar**

weather = **el tiempo**

wedding = **la boda**

when = **cuando**

white = **blanco**

winter = **el invierno**

writer = **el/la escritor/a**

Appendix C

Common Irregular Present and Past Participles

• •

*P*resent and past participles can come in handy, but the irregular present and past participles often are difficult to remember. To help keep them fresh in your mind, this appendix provides a brief overview of common irregular present and past participles.

Eying Irregular Present Participles

You form the present participle (*ing* ending in English) regularly in Spanish by doing the following:

✔ Dropping the **-ar** off of an **-ar** verb and adding **-ando**

   mirar (to look at, watch) becomes **mirando** (watching)

✔ Dropping the **-er** or **-ir** off of **-er** or **-ir** verbs and adding **-iendo**

   comer (to eat) becomes **comiendo** (eating)

   escribir (to write) becomes **escribiendo** (writing)

These rules do have a few exceptions.

The most common irregular present participles are listed in the table that follows.

Verb	Translation	Present Participle	Translation
caer	to fall	cayendo	falling
conseguir	to attain, achieve	consiguiendo	attaining, achieving
construir	to construct	construyendo	constructing
creer	to believe	creyendo	believing
decir	to say, tell	diciendo	saying, telling
divertirse	to enjoy oneself	divirtiéndose	enjoying oneself
dormir	to sleep	durmiendo	sleeping
ir	to go	yendo	going
leer	to read	leyendo	reading
oír	to hear	oyendo	hearing

(continued)

Verb	Translation	Present Participle	Translation
pedir	to ask for, to request	pidiendo	asking for, requesting
poder	to be able	pudiendo	being able
repetir	to repeat	repitiendo	repeating
seguir	to follow	siguiendo	following
servir	to serve	sirviendo	serving
traer	to bring	trayendo	bringing
venir	to come	viniendo	coming
vestirse	to get dressed	vistiéndose	getting dressed

Getting a Grip on Irregular Past Participles

You form the past participle (-ed ending in English) for regular verbs in Spanish by doing the following:

✓ Dropping the -ar off of an -ar verb and adding -ado

   hablar (to speak) becomes hablado (spoken)

✓ Dropping the -er or -ir off of an -er or -ir verb and adding -ido

   vender (to sell) becomes vendido (sold)

   salir (to leave) becomes salido (left)

The most common irregular past participles are listed in the table that follows.

Verb	Translation	Past Participle	Translation
abrir	to open	abierto	opened
caer	to fall	caído	fallen
creer	to believe	creído	believed
cubrir	to cover	cubierto	covered
decir	to say, tell	dicho	said, told
descubrir	to discover	descubierto	discovered
devolver	to return (something)	devuelto	returned (something)
escribir	to write	escrito	written
hacer	to do, make	hecho	done, made
ir	to go	ido	gone
leer	to read	leído	read
morir	to die	muerto	died
oír	to hear	oído	heard

Verb	Translation	Past Participle	Translation
poner	to put	puesto	put
reír	to laugh	reído	laughed
resolver	to resolve	resuelto	resolved
romper	to break	roto	broken
sonreír	to smile	sonreído	smiled
traer	to bring	traído	brought
ver	to see	visto	seen
volver	to return	vuelto	returned

Index

BUSINESS, CAREERS & PERSONAL FINANCE

0-7645-5307-0

0-7645-5331-3 *†

Also available:

- Accounting For Dummies †
  0-7645-5314-3
- Business Plans Kit For Dummies †
  0-7645-5365-8
- Cover Letters For Dummies
  0-7645-5224-4
- Frugal Living For Dummies
  0-7645-5403-4
- Leadership For Dummies
  0-7645-5176-0
- Managing For Dummies
  0-7645-1771-6

- Marketing For Dummies
  0-7645-5600-2
- Personal Finance For Dummies *
  0-7645-2590-5
- Project Management For Dummies
  0-7645-5283-X
- Resumes For Dummies †
  0-7645-5471-9
- Selling For Dummies
  0-7645-5363-1
- Small Business Kit For Dummies *†
  0-7645-5093-4

HOME & BUSINESS COMPUTER BASICS

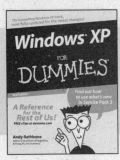

0-7645-4074-2

0-7645-3758-X

Also available:

- ACT! 6 For Dummies
  0-7645-2645-6
- iLife '04 All-in-One Desk Reference
  For Dummies
  0-7645-7347-0
- iPAQ For Dummies
  0-7645-6769-1
- Mac OS X Panther Timesaving
  Techniques For Dummies
  0-7645-5812-9
- Macs For Dummies
  0-7645-5656-8
- Microsoft Money 2004 For Dummies
  0-7645-4195-1

- Office 2003 All-in-One Desk Reference
  For Dummies
  0-7645-3883-7
- Outlook 2003 For Dummies
  0-7645-3759-8
- PCs For Dummies
  0-7645-4074-2
- TiVo For Dummies
  0-7645-6923-6
- Upgrading and Fixing PCs For Dummies
  0-7645-1665-5
- Windows XP Timesaving Techniques
  For Dummies
  0-7645-3748-2

FOOD, HOME, GARDEN, HOBBIES, MUSIC & PETS

0-7645-5295-3

0-7645-5232-5

Also available:

- Bass Guitar For Dummies
  0-7645-2487-9
- Diabetes Cookbook For Dummies
  0-7645-5230-9
- Gardening For Dummies *
  0-7645-5130-2
- Guitar For Dummies
  0-7645-5106-X
- Holiday Decorating For Dummies
  0-7645-2570-0
- Home Improvement All-in-One
  For Dummies
  0-7645-5680-0

- Knitting For Dummies
  0-7645-5395-X
- Piano For Dummies
  0-7645-5105-1
- Puppies For Dummies
  0-7645-5255-4
- Scrapbooking For Dummies
  0-7645-7208-3
- Senior Dogs For Dummies
  0-7645-5818-8
- Singing For Dummies
  0-7645-2475-5
- 30-Minute Meals For Dummies
  0-7645-2589-1

INTERNET & DIGITAL MEDIA

0-7645-1664-7

0-7645-6924-4

Also available:

- 2005 Online Shopping Directory
  For Dummies
  0-7645-7495-7
- CD & DVD Recording For Dummies
  0-7645-5956-7
- eBay For Dummies
  0-7645-5654-1
- Fighting Spam For Dummies
  0-7645-5965-6
- Genealogy Online For Dummies
  0-7645-5964-8
- Google For Dummies
  0-7645-4420-9

- Home Recording For Musicians
  For Dummies
  0-7645-1634-5
- The Internet For Dummies
  0-7645-4173-0
- iPod & iTunes For Dummies
  0-7645-7772-7
- Preventing Identity Theft For Dummies
  0-7645-7336-5
- Pro Tools All-in-One Desk Reference
  For Dummies
  0-7645-5714-9
- Roxio Easy Media Creator For Dummies
  0-7645-7131-1

* Separate Canadian edition also available
† Separate U.K. edition also available

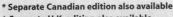

Available wherever books are sold. For more information or to order direct: U.S. customers visit www.dummies.com or call 1-877-762-2974.
U.K. customers visit www.wileyeurope.com or call 0800 243407. Canadian customers visit www.wiley.ca or call 1-800-567-4797.

SPORTS, FITNESS, PARENTING, RELIGION & SPIRITUALITY

0-7645-5146-9

0-7645-5418-2

Also available:
- Adoption For Dummies
  0-7645-5488-3
- Basketball For Dummies
  0-7645-5248-1
- The Bible For Dummies
  0-7645-5296-1
- Buddhism For Dummies
  0-7645-5359-3
- Catholicism For Dummies
  0-7645-5391-7
- Hockey For Dummies
  0-7645-5228-7

- Judaism For Dummies
  0-7645-5299-6
- Martial Arts For Dummies
  0-7645-5358-5
- Pilates For Dummies
  0-7645-5397-6
- Religion For Dummies
  0-7645-5264-3
- Teaching Kids to Read For Dummies
  0-7645-4043-2
- Weight Training For Dummies
  0-7645-5168-X
- Yoga For Dummies
  0-7645-5117-5

TRAVEL

0-7645-5438-7

0-7645-5453-0

Also available:
- Alaska For Dummies
  0-7645-1761-9
- Arizona For Dummies
  0-7645-6938-4
- Cancún and the Yucatán For Dummies
  0-7645-2437-2
- Cruise Vacations For Dummies
  0-7645-6941-4
- Europe For Dummies
  0-7645-5456-5
- Ireland For Dummies
  0-7645-5455-7

- Las Vegas For Dummies
  0-7645-5448-4
- London For Dummies
  0-7645-4277-X
- New York City For Dummies
  0-7645-6945-7
- Paris For Dummies
  0-7645-5494-8
- RV Vacations For Dummies
  0-7645-5443-3
- Walt Disney World & Orlando For Dummies
  0-7645-6943-0

GRAPHICS, DESIGN & WEB DEVELOPMENT

0-7645-4345-8

0-7645-5589-8

Also available:
- Adobe Acrobat 6 PDF For Dummies
  0-7645-3760-1
- Building a Web Site For Dummies
  0-7645-7144-3
- Dreamweaver MX 2004 For Dummies
  0-7645-4342-3
- FrontPage 2003 For Dummies
  0-7645-3882-9
- HTML 4 For Dummies
  0-7645-1995-6
- Illustrator CS For Dummies
  0-7645-4084-X

- Macromedia Flash MX 2004 For Dummies
  0-7645-4358-X
- Photoshop 7 All-in-One Desk Reference
  For Dummies
  0-7645-1667-1
- Photoshop CS Timesaving Techniques
  For Dummies
  0-7645-6782-9
- PHP 5 For Dummies
  0-7645-4166-8
- PowerPoint 2003 For Dummies
  0-7645-3908-6
- QuarkXPress 6 For Dummies
  0-7645-2593-X

NETWORKING, SECURITY, PROGRAMMING & DATABASES

0-7645-6852-3

0-7645-5784-X

Also available:
- A+ Certification For Dummies
  0-7645-4187-0
- Access 2003 All-in-One Desk Reference
  For Dummies
  0-7645-3988-4
- Beginning Programming For Dummies
  0-7645-4997-9
- C For Dummies
  0-7645-7068-4
- Firewalls For Dummies
  0-7645-4048-3
- Home Networking For Dummies
  0-7645-42796

- Network Security For Dummies
  0-7645-1679-5
- Networking For Dummies
  0-7645-1677-9
- TCP/IP For Dummies
  0-7645-1760-0
- VBA For Dummies
  0-7645-3989-2
- Wireless All In-One Desk Reference
  For Dummies
  0-7645-7496-5
- Wireless Home Networking For Dummies
  0-7645-3910-8

HEALTH & SELF-HELP

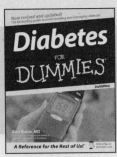

0-7645-6820-5 *†

0-7645-2566-2

Also available:

- Alzheimer's For Dummies
  0-7645-3899-3
- Asthma For Dummies
  0-7645-4233-8
- Controlling Cholesterol For Dummies
  0-7645-5440-9
- Depression For Dummies
  0-7645-3900-0
- Dieting For Dummies
  0-7645-4149-8
- Fertility For Dummies
  0-7645-2549-2
- Fibromyalgia For Dummies
  0-7645-5441-7

- Improving Your Memory For Dummies
  0-7645-5435-2
- Pregnancy For Dummies †
  0-7645-4483-7
- Quitting Smoking For Dummies
  0-7645-2629-4
- Relationships For Dummies
  0-7645-5384-4
- Thyroid For Dummies
  0-7645-5385-2

EDUCATION, HISTORY, REFERENCE & TEST PREPARATION

0-7645-5194-9

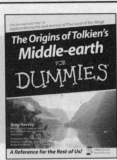

0-7645-4186-2

Also available:

- Algebra For Dummies
  0-7645-5325-9
- British History For Dummies
  0-7645-7021-8
- Calculus For Dummies
  0-7645-2498-4
- English Grammar For Dummies
  0-7645-5322-4
- Forensics For Dummies
  0-7645-5580-4
- The GMAT For Dummies
  0-7645-5251-1
- Inglés Para Dummies
  0-7645-5427-1

- Italian For Dummies
  0-7645-5196-5
- Latin For Dummies
  0-7645-5431-X
- Lewis & Clark For Dummies
  0-7645-2545-X
- Research Papers For Dummies
  0-7645-5426-3
- The SAT I For Dummies
  0-7645-7193-1
- Science Fair Projects For Dummies
  0-7645-5460-3
- U.S. History For Dummies
  0-7645-5249-X

Get smart @ dummies.com®

- **Find a full list of Dummies titles**
- **Look into loads of FREE on-site articles**
- **Sign up for FREE eTips e-mailed to you weekly**
- **See what other products carry the Dummies name**
- **Shop directly from the Dummies bookstore**
- **Enter to win new prizes every month!**

* Separate Canadian edition also available
† Separate U.K. edition also available

Available wherever books are sold. For more information or to order direct: U.S. customers visit www.dummies.com or call 1-877-762-2974.
U.K. customers visit www.wileyeurope.com or call 0800 243407. Canadian customers visit www.wiley.ca or call 1-800-567-4797.